Stories of God's great faithfulness
in the lives of His children

Compiled & told by
Tammy Sumner

Foreword by Aaron Wilburn
Conclusion by Lynda Randle

Printed in the United States of America

Unless otherwise stated, scripture is taken from the King James Version Bible (Public Domain)

ISBN: 978-0-578-60621-7 (Paperback)

Stories were submitted for publishing by individual writers with written consent to publish. The writers are free to share, publish, and reuse their own stories at their own discretion without penalty of law.

Front/back cover image by Kevin Carden, used by permission.
Book design by Sumwhatsouth Design, Sumwhatsouth.com

Lily of the Valley Publishing, Inc.
Santa Claus, Indiana 47579 USA
PH: 812.661.1323

mylilyofthevalley.org
publishing@mylilyofthevalley.org

CONTENTS

FOREWORD

A FAITHFUL FATHER

"FAITHFUL FATHER, FAITHFUL FATHER,
YOU'VE ALWAYS BEEN, YOU'LL ALWAYS BE
FAITHFUL TO ME.....
FAITHFUL FATHER, FAITHFUL FATHER...
YOU'VE ALWAYS BEEN, YOU'LL ALWAYS BE
FAITHFUL TO ME..."

-words and music Tim Parton, and C. Aaron Wilburn

This is the simple chorus of a song recently written with Tim Parton for a children's project for the 3ABN television network. When asked to write a children's project and include a song about God's faithfulness, it came so easy.

If you want to know all about a town or community, ask the woman or man who has spent their years there; they will be happy to tell you about the joys and the tough times where they have lived.

If you want to know about the character of our Heavenly Father, His devotion, and dependability, his loving-kindness, and care for His children, ask the man who has leaned on Him for seventy years.... the woman who has trusted Him to meet her needs since she was widowed 50 years ago; from these lips, you will hear truth. Look into those eyes as they shine, telling you about the times only God could do what He did.... the prayers that were answered when situations looked hopeless. I have never asked an elderly child of God to describe Him when I was disappointed in the answer!

Not only do I know God is faithful because of their stories and testimonies, but I have also found Him faithful to me. When I was 16, I walked into Virginia Boulevard Church of God in Huntsville, Alabama, at the invitation of my friends, Elmer "Red" and Nelda Lewis......this Freewill Baptist boy was nervous...I'd heard about "these" people!! Walking down the aisle of the church, I was stopped by the sound of a man snapping his fingers as he said, "*stop right there, young man.*" I looked to my left to see a blind man pointing at me, Uncle Joe Wilbanks. He said, "*I don't know who you are, I don't know your name, but the Spirit of the Lord has just told me to tell you---He has anointed you to write songs, and your songs will be heard around the world.*" Months later, I was hospitalized, and my parents were told that I would not survive. My mom sat beside my bed after being told to contact the rest of the family and friends, and she prayed to the faithful God she had served so many years.

Today, I feel like my songs... *What A Beautiful Day for the Lord to Come Again, That Sounds Like Home to Me, It's Beginning to Rain, Four Days Late*, and many more, are not just songs--but testimonies that God is faithful!

His word is true, and if He has spoken it, He will see it through. That is *truth* for the young and the old, and all in between...

"He's always been... He'll always be.... faithful to me... He's a faithful Father."

This book is the result of people saying... "*we want to hear more about the faithfulness of God.*" -More everyday encounters in the lives of believers who have come face to face, not only with the hand of God, but the experience of knowing His love, His compassion, and His loving kindness.

This book is a collection of the faithfulness of One who hears and sees, knows, and understands. This book is only a drink from the ocean that is His devotion to His creation.

Some wonderful friends have shared in this book, their struggles, their doubts, pain, fear, and losses--as well as heartwarming encounters with the Father who has provided peace in troubled times, hope when the tomb was sealed, and life on the other side of—"it's too late now."

As you read, our prayer is that you will see yourself in the pages and be reminded again and again

"You've always been, you'll always be... faithful to me."

-Aaron Wilburn
songwriter, humorist,
singer, speaker

ACKNOWLEDGMENTS

Before these stories, and before the idea of a book was even conceived, God had a plan. So, to Him goes the first note of thanks and acknowledgement that, without Him, there would be no stories.

"If in this life only we have hope in Christ, we are of all men most miserable." 1 Corinthians 15:19

This book would not have been possible without the support and encouragement of my husband, Curtis Sumner. His research and organizational skills were invaluable, as was his willingness to jump in to help with whatever task I had to let go to work on the book!

Thank you to Lauren Sumner for her extensive book knowledge; your love for books is one of the many things I love about you! A special thanks to Chandler Sumner for his patience with me as I juggled one too many things, I am so blessed to be your mom!

Thank you to my friend, Johnathan Bond, for planting the idea of putting my stories into a book. I hope my stories inspire others as much as yours inspire me!

Words cannot express my gratitude to Editor, Amy Boll, for her endless hours of reading, editing, and for her friendship.

Last, but certainly not least, thank you to everyone who wrote their stories for this book. Because of your faithfulness, I know many will be blessed, encouraged, and will come to know the powerful God we serve!

INTRODUCTION

Since I was a child, I have sensed God's hand in my life. In my early years, amidst trauma and fear, He was my protector. When faced with certain death, He was my deliverer. And, when my family was without a place to go and down to our last pack of crackers, He was our miraculous provider!

Just as I have seen God's hand guiding me through my life, I have also witnessed His grace and mercy woven like a beautiful tapestry through the lives of my friends and loved ones. We serve a God who is not bound by our mortal limitations and who loves and cares for us and wants to have a relationship with us. Oh yes, He is faithful… even when we are not!

For years, our family ministry, *Faithful Crossings*, has traveled the US, singing and telling our personal stories of God's great faithfulness and love for His children. Many of our stories have been the inspiration behind the songs we sing, and many have resonated with people from all walks of life and all circumstances. These stories have been requested many times in some written or recorded form so that people can share them with friends and loved ones. That's how this book began, but, as usual, God had bigger plans than I did. As I began to write and compile the memories and moments that were so dear to me, I began to feel God's nudging to reach out to family and friends and even other artists, writers, and ministries so they could tell their stories too. What evolved was a beautiful outpouring of testimonies of God's faithfulness from all over the country!

I believe that no matter what you are facing right now, God has a story in this book just for you. My prayer is that you find comfort, reassurance, and, most of all, HOPE in knowing that God loves you, He cares for you, and He never abandons His own.

-Tammy Sumner
Faithful Crossings

1

GOD JUST SHOWED UP!

Kathy Murphy

God is Faithful. Several years ago, my husband Dennis and I lived in Minnesota, but our family all lived in St. Louis. On holidays and special occasions, we would travel south to celebrate and visit. My children had all moved back to St. Louis to start their families, and I was in a depression that only women that have experienced an "empty nest" can truly understand.

I was looking forward to seeing my children and grandchildren, who hold a very special place in my heart. As is typical with pastors of small churches, we were struggling financially and probably shouldn't have tried to make the trip. It was Christmastime, and I really wanted to be with my family. Driving through Minnesota and Iowa can be especially harrowing in the winter. We had been driving through bitter cold and snow for about six hours when we decided to stop for the night to rest and get off the highway in Cedar Rapids, which is halfway to St. Louis from our home in Minnesota.

After a good night's sleep, we got up early to continue the trip. It was Christmas Eve, and we really wanted to make it there before evening. It was extremely cold in Iowa, and all kinds of weather records had been broken overnight. I think the wind chill was -35 with a temperature of about -10. We had been driving for about 10 minutes when the car started shaking and coughing, making a horrible noise. We got off at the first exit at a little gas station with an A&W attached to it. The car stopped there and wouldn't go any further as it spewed out all kinds of stuff from the tailpipe and engine.

Apparently, my husband didn't check the anti-freeze, and the radiator was cracked. I was beyond frustrated, and I was really upset at my man. While he was trying to pour things into the engine, I was sitting in the extremely cold car, but my anger was so hot that I didn't even feel the temperature! I started to cry and pray and ask God, "*Now what?*" We had no extra money to spend on car repairs, let alone funds for another night at the hotel. Since it was Christmas Eve, there was hardly anything open in Cedar Rapids, and no one that would be able to tow us.

I was sitting in the extremely cold car, but my anger was so hot that I didn't even feel the temperature!

Our daughter is married to a very talented man who can fix anything mechanically. He would be the guy you would want with you during a disaster. He can figure out anything, so my husband called him to get advice. My son-in-law, Larry, is a great man but was on the fence about Christianity. We were the only Bible he read. When Dennis told him what was going on, he snidely remarked, "*Where is your God now?*"

My son in law said he would make a few calls and maybe drive up to get us. While we were waiting and pondering what to do, Dennis remembered that a church member's parents, Jerry and Gwen, lived in Cedar Rapids. We had met them before (that is another story for another time) so, Dennis called Jerry and explained our situation. Jerry told Dennis that he would call him back, that he had something to do. About 10 minutes later, Jerry called and told us that a tow truck was on its way. He had also rented us a car for a few days, and he was going to have the car repaired! He said he would be there to pick us up and we were going to have lunch with him and Gwen.

---

he snidely remarked,

"Where is your God now?"

Jerry explained to us that, right before Dennis called him, he and Gwen were having a conversation about a bonus that she received from work, and they wanted to bless someone with their abundance. When Dennis called, he and Gwen knew that it was a "God thing," and they knew that is how they were supposed to spend her bonus.

It has always been so hard for me to accept any gift or help from anyone. When I protested, Jerry told me that I would be taking away the blessing they were receiving for helping us. We were so humbled and thankful for their generosity! This wasn't a small gift! They put a new engine in our car, paid for towing, and sent us on our way with a rental car (which, by the way, was the same make and model as our car, except newer).

Within two hours, we were on our way to spend Christmas with our family. Dennis called to tell my daughter what had happened. When Larry, her husband, answered the phone. Dennis said to him, "*God just showed up*."

2

OBEDIENCE BRINGS AN OFFERING

Adam Borden

When I got my first gig playing bass for a group with a bus in 1991, I promptly emptied all my savings and sock drawer money and drove to a music store called Rhythm City that used to be in downtown Atlanta. Hanging on the wall was an amber-colored five-string Michael V. Pedulla brand bass, which would become my constant companion for decades ahead in studios and on stages all over the world. It was my main bass for the 10+ years as I played as a member of Gold City's band, *The Band of Gold.*

Even though my opportunities to play bass as a sideman were much fewer over the years, I still hung on to that bass. It became an heirloom that would someday be passed down. I had never considered getting rid of the Pedulla. I only came close in July of 2014 when my wife, Angel, was diagnosed with breast cancer. Money was tighter than ever, and the mounting medical bills were putting us in a bad position. We had some hard choices to make.

I sent out a message to some of my musician friends explaining the situation. I let them know that I was going to sell the Pedulla, but I wanted it to go to someone who would appreciate it. Within minutes I received a call from my long-time friend, Jeff Easter, who advised me that he wasn't going to let me sell that bass. He had already called a few of our friends, and they were making up my asking price to send us for the medical bills so I could keep the Pedulla. Needless to say, that act of friendship was very special to me. The Lord let me keep the Pedulla, a part of Angel's medical bills was paid, and God got the glory.

Later, when Angel was in the middle of her chemotherapy treatment, we were out of money and had no one else to turn to. Our church, friends, and family had been very generous, but we were completely tapped out. We had a balance of $500 at the cancer treatment center, and if we could not catch up the balance by 5:00 PM on a certain date, Angel would have to suspend her treatments. We prayed and prayed. All we had was the Lord, and if He did not come through, we were sunk. This was not just an overdue bill; Angel's life hung in the balance.

The due date arrived, and no solution had been found. After work that day, we brought the girls home from school and headed inside the house. It was 4:45 PM. I didn't want to go inside that house. I just kept wanting to believe that the Lord was going to come through somehow, some way. I headed to the mailbox expecting to find more medical statements and bills. Sure enough, the mailbox was stuffed with the usual filler, except for one item. I found an envelope with the return address of Cullman, Alabama, and my cousin's name, Clay Borden. We had not seen Clay and his family for a couple of years since we had been living in Florida. I walked inside and began to open the envelope expecting to find a card with well wishes and prayers, but there was something more. As I opened the card, out came a Visa gift card for $500! It was exactly what we needed to pay the outstanding balance! We all burst into tears. Angel dialed the cancer treatment center, and through her tears, she gave the payment information. The payment came, Angel completed her treatment, and God got the glory.

As that young preacher preached the paint off the walls, the Holy Spirit began to speak to my heart.

Fast forward 28 years after I plunked down my hard-earned cash for the Pedulla in 1991. Today, I am 14 years removed from life as a full-time traveling musician. It's been ten years since I surrendered to preach, and now, I am 3 years along in the call to evangelism.

Saturday morning, January 26th of 2019, found me on the platform seated beside the piano and the Pedulla listening to a young fireball preacher named Dr. Justin Cooper at the Wahoo Baptist Church's winter youth meeting in Cleveland, Georgia. More than 2000 young people and pastors sang Red-Book and Southern Gospel songs from memory and listened with hungry hearts to the man of God preach the Word from the King James Bible. His message from Numbers and Joshua was titled, "*Sorry, Aaron, all you get is God.*"

As that young preacher preached the paint off the walls, the Holy Spirit began to speak to my heart. "*Take that bass, lay it on the altar, and await instructions.*" "*Yes, Sir,*" was my answer. By this time, many others were already in the altar while Bro. Cooper preached. I laid the Pedulla face down on the outer mourner's bench and crumbled into the altar to listen to the Spirit's instruction. "*Leave the bass there, sell it, and give the money to that young preacher.*" "*Yes, Sir,*" was my answer.

I made my way back around to my seat on the platform and motioned for my pastor, Brother Mark Stroud. I told him what the Lord had told me to do. He asked if I was sure. "*Yes, sell it and give the money to that preacher.*" He asked how much it might be worth. I advised a brand new one just like it would go for about $5000, but a used one could be had for about $2000.

At the end of the service, Brother Stroud addressed the crowd and told them what the Lord had told me to do; "*Sell the bass, give the money to Brother Cooper.*" A pastor friend of mine named Doug Raynes spoke up and asked if the folks in attendance could redeem the bass by giving an offering for Brother Cooper and giving the Pedulla back to me. Almost instantly, people were bringing cash and checks and laying them on the altar. When it was all said and done, Brother Cooper brought the bass from the altar and laid it in my lap, and the Lord gave him an offering of over $5000. That's the equivalent of the full price of a brand new Pedulla bass!

1 Samuel 15:22 says, "*...to obey is greater than sacrifice...*" The fruit of true sacrificial obedience that is grounded in faith is that others get blessed, you get blessed, and God gets the glory. On that Saturday, Brother Cooper got a great offering, I got the Pedulla back, and God got the glory.

3

THE ELEVENTH HOUR

Penny Cook

Once, during my faith-growing time, when I was single with three children, I had a desperate financial need. I asked the Lord to help me with this need, but it seemed as though my prayers were falling on deaf ears. I worked extra, scrimped every penny, but still did not have enough for the need. When the day came that the bill had to be paid, I was still short what I needed. Late in the afternoon, I was crying out to God and telling him that I could not understand why it seemed that He had not helped me.

"*I have worked and saved and continued to pay my tithes. I have stood on your Word and proclaimed to others that you would help me. I know that Your Word is true and that You are not a man who will lie. And I know that you always provide, so I'm going to stand on that Word*".

About that time, the phone rang. It was the secretary of our church. She began to apologize, but I didn't understand for what. She said, "*I left to go on vacation a month ago, and there was a check on my desk for you. I told the person who covered for me that it was there and to call you. It got covered with some other papers and then she forgot about it. I just found it on my desk when I was cleaning it off.*" It was just the amount I needed, and I had just enough time to go get the check, cash it, and cover the need!

What the Lord showed me through that was that He had provided for the need a month ago. Through a series of circumstances (of which no one did anything wrong), it just had been delayed. I would have been appreciative if I had gotten the check when it was first sent to me, but I would not have learned the lesson of God's timing and knowing that He ALWAYS provides. Sometimes we just don't receive it until what seems to us is the eleventh hour. The greater lesson was that He is ALWAYS Faithful, and He ALWAYS provides for His children. He's a Good, Good Father. He is indeed Jehovah Jireh – God, our Provider, but, in HIS timing and HIS way - not necessarily ours. He is wise. He knows what we need so much more than we do. Trust Him. He always does what is best.

4

FROM FEAR TO FORGIVENESS

Tammy Sumner

I remember that day well. We were sitting in the den when a car pulled into that old gravel driveway, and mom said, "Tammy, run!" We had practiced it time and time again. I'd run to my room, lock my door, and hide and I wouldn't come out until mom said it was safe. I can remember locking my door behind me and hiding behind the thin, white curtains in my bedroom. I could hear a commotion in the hallway outside my door and the sobbing and pleading of my mom, and I knew they wanted in. I ran from the curtains and darted quickly underneath my bed and held my breath, hoping they'd leave, but they didn't.

After what felt like forever, I heard my mom say, "Tammy, baby, unlock the door and come out." She was crying; I knew something was wrong. I didn't want to leave the safety of my bedroom. I was confused and scared, but, eventually, I did as I was told.

My world came crashing down that day, and this is the story of how God put it all back together again.

That was just a short snapshot from the timeline of my early childhood. I was only eight months old when I came to live with my grandparents. Days turned into weeks, and weeks turned into months and, eventually, they became "mom and dad" to me. I now had a family that loved me with brothers and a sister, too; life was good, and we were happy.

I never knew my birth mother, and even though my birth-father had rarely visited me over the past few years, the failing court system granted him partial custody of me when I was only four years old. What followed was me being taken away to a place where no one knew where I was. A little trailer in rural Alabama is where I would spend the next week or so of my life. In the daytime, I would be mistreated by the older stepchild that also lived in the trailer. At night, as I would cry for the only mommy I had ever known, I would be told that she was dead and that I would never see her again; then, I'd be beaten until I couldn't cry anymore.

As a child, I would sleep with
my hands placed on my mom's cheeks,
in fear that I might be taken away again
in the middle of the night

My family never stopped loving me or looking for me. My brother, Roger, left home and told my mom and dad that he wouldn't be back until he found me, and that's exactly what he did. When I arrived back home, I was in such a state of shock that the doctors said I might never recover. But, once again, they loved me and nursed me back to health and, most importantly, they took me to church and told me about Jesus, the Father who would always be there for me and who would always be faithful.

I grew up being deathly afraid of my birth-father. I was so afraid of him that I let it rule my life. As a child, I would sleep with my hands placed on my mom's cheeks, in fear that I might be taken away again in the middle of the night. As I grew up, I could never go on field trips without a special chaperone or spend the night at a friend's house. Sometimes, we'd be driving down the road, and it would seem we were being followed, so we'd have to speed to the nearest police station to safety, sometimes almost wrecking our car in the process.

Yes, fear ruled my life. This fear followed me well into my adult years. I was married and expecting our first child when my boss told me I was going to have to take a business trip to Colorado. I didn't know much about my birth father, but I knew that he lived somewhere in Colorado. I was terrified. I fought with all my being to keep from going on that business trip. I even explained that if I had to quit my job to keep from going to Colorado, I would do just that. Finally, they decided that they would send someone else, and I could relax; I would be safe.

What I got back was the sweetest, kindest letter of love and apology that I could have ever imagined

---

Fast-forward to Father's Day of 2005. We had moved to Minnesota- far away from the home I grew up in and far away from Colorado. We were in church that Sunday morning, listening to a special Father's Day message about our Heavenly Father, and about forgiveness. I don't remember very much of that sermon, but I remember my heart nearly beating out of my chest. At that moment, I knew I was supposed to contact this man I had lived in fear of my whole life and offer forgiveness.

When the invitation was given, I went up to the front and prayed and told God that I would do whatever He wanted me to do. On the way home, I talked with Curtis about this decision. With wide eyes, he simply said, "*Tammy, that's a big decision. How about praying about it, and if it's really God's will, He will reveal it to you.*" I agreed, and that night before bed, as promised, I prayed for guidance and for reassurance that I was doing the right thing.

Early the next morning, I was awakened by the phone ringing. It was my sister on the other line; she was calling because she had found the address for my birth father and felt that God was leading her to give it to me. With tears, she told me she loved me and that she would love me no matter what I chose to do with that address and that we would always be sisters, this was my answer.

Later that week, I was able to use the mailing address she'd given me to find a website and email address for him online. I took a few days to build up the courage to write that first letter and prayed over it before hitting the "send" button. What I got back was the sweetest, kindest letter of love and apology that I could have ever imagined. Soon, there was a phone call and, eventually, a trip to Colorado to spend a weekend with this man that I had feared my whole life. Gone was the fear that I had lived in for so long. Gone was the anger that had built up inside me for so many years. ONLY GOD can do this!

Through the next 10+ years, we kept in touch with an occasional phone call or a short visit. Then, in December of 2016, we got the call that he was in the hospital, nearing the end of his life. We were able to go and spend some of his last days by his side. I stood at his bedside and prayed over him and sang the song, *"It's Not a Miracle to God."*

Maybe it's you who needs a miracle today. I am so thankful that God's grace and mercy doesn't just extend to those who are worthy because the Bible says that "ALL have sinned and fall short of the Glory of God" it also says that our "righteousness is as filthy rags." So, rest assured today, you are loved. You are precious. You are worth rescuing from whatever situation you find yourself in; won't you give that situation to God and let Him work it out?

Tammy with Larry on her 2005 visit to Colorado

5

GOD HAD DIFFERENT PLANS!

Lisa Cox

It was a typical weekday morning in 2007. We were getting our six-year-old daughter, Callie, ready for school, so my husband, Jamie, and I thought we would let our 18-month-old son, Tucker, sleep. When I went into his room to rouse him, he wouldn't wake up; I shook him, but he was limp and unresponsive! He began to convulse and then started turning blue. We called 911, and they arrived within a couple of minutes. They carried his little lifeless body into the ambulance and said that only one of us could ride, so I hopped on.

It was all a blur, but I do clearly remember, as they were giving him rescue breaths, laying my hands on him and praying. I asked God to spare our son's life and heal whatever was wrong with him. The paramedics got him into the emergency room, and the doctors continued to work on him. He began to gain consciousness. We were very concerned but very relieved that he had been revived!

The doctor was still very concerned that there could be brain damage and feared he was not out of the woods. She called in the Flight for Life and had him flown to Cardinal Glennon Children's Hospital in St. Louis. They said there was no room for anyone to ride on the helicopter, so my husband and I drove the two-hour trip (which seemed like an eternity). After tests, exams, and a night in the hospital, they released our son to go home. They said that not only was there no brain damage, but they had no explanation of the events that had taken place because he was perfectly healthy.

A couple of months later, I ran into one of the paramedics who was in the ambulance with us, and he recognized me. He looked surprised that I had a little toddler running alongside me. He said, "*I was certain that the baby I was dropping off that morning wasn't going to make it.*" I just smiled and thought, "*God had different plans.*" We know the explanation; our Mighty Father's intervening hand chose to spare our son. Tucker is now fourteen and is a healthy, strong, and loving boy who is thriving. We thank God every day for the loving protection and provision that He provides our family.

6

WHAT DO THEY DO?

Rick Alan King

On September 25, 2003, at 10:20 PM, I received a telephone call that would forever change me and my wife's life. Many of you might remember the tragic fire at NHC Nursing Home in Nashville that claimed the lives of 16 of their residents, one of them being my mother-in-law.

My wife, Lana, and I had just returned from our daily visit when the phone rang, and it was my mother-in-law screaming, "*Baby, come save me. The place is on fire, and I can't walk!*" I could hear the alarms and screaming going on in the background. She could no longer get out of bed and walk due to her spinal problems. We immediately took off as fast as we could and arrived before many of the emergency personnel even got there.

We tried to get into the building to help but could not. We stood outside and watched, hoped, and prayed as the firemen were doing all they could to rescue the residents. We comforted people as they brought them out to the triage area wrapped in sheets, blankets, and some with nothing on at all.

They were very scared but would seem to calm down when they saw us as we were regular visitors and familiar faces.

As the evening wore on, my wife had to return to the car as she has COPD and is on oxygen and was too tired to help anymore. I continued to search, walk around, and ask anyone of the whereabouts of my mother-in-law, but no one knew anything. By this time there were countless fire trucks, ambulances, police, helicopters and news media with cameras and cords spread out over the entire area and as I stood there amongst the chaos looking up at the smoldering building, I could not help but hear and notice many people passing all around me who were very angry and many even cursing about the events taking place. All I could think of was, "*God, please help us, help us all.*"

It was my mother-in-law screaming,

"Baby, come save me.

The place is on fire, and I can't walk!"

While I stood there, lost in thought, I felt something brush my hand. I turned to look at what it was, and it was a sweet little elderly black lady with a gray bun on her head and a smile on her face. She looked directly at me and said, "*Baby, aren't you glad you are a Christian?*" and I said, "*Yes*," and turned back around to the scenes that were unfolding at the time. She then said about the people that were cursing and angry all around us, "*What do they do, who do they turn to?*" I then turned around to reply to her, and she was gone, vanished in an instant. There was that word again, "Baby." My mother-in-law had never called me that before that night.

Those words, "*What do they do, who do they turn to?*" never left my mind. It wasn't until I had to bury my precious mother, less than a year later, that those words came racing into my mind again, and I was more glad than ever that I had someone to turn to for comfort.

I sat down after that, and it started flowing out of me; the words and music to my song that I perform at every venue I play. The chorus to the song says, "What do they do without Him, how do they live without Him, when troubles come, when day is done, do they just hide or run?, How do they live without Him, what do they do without Him, I only know I just can't make it on my own."

7

THE PORTA-POTTY STORY

Carla Harris Justice

I hate Porta-Potties! It all started back in the late 70's when I took my daughter, Jana, to see the group Alabama's June Jam in Fort Payne. While in a Porta Potty for the first time, I got locked in and couldn't get out. I told Jana, who was standing outside waiting on me, to go get help. Needless to say, I hate them!

In 2005, I was hired by CrossPoint Community Church to be the Director of Jail Ministries. That year, I took my 4-year-old granddaughter, Savana, to Trunk or Treat at the church. Being a wise grandmother, I asked Savana if she needed to use the Porta-Potty. She didn't, but I thought I would because we were up at the front of the line, and it had not been used much. I told her to stand outside and wait for me. WOW! Porta-Potties have really been updated since I was in the one at June Jam. Outside are different colors, a light comes on, and there are liners for the seats. WOW! I was impressed.

Being a cool night, I had worn a sweatshirt and sweatpants. My sweatpants didn't have pockets, so I had stuck my keys in the back of my pants' waistband. As I sat down, I heard a loud "KER-PLUMP," I thought, "OH NO, I

DIDN'T!" I could call the maintenance crew or CrossPoint Staff to get my keys out. But, OH, NO! I would never hear the end of it. What was I going to do?

First of all, I raised my sweatshirt sleeve as far as it would go so that I could reach down in the pot. Surely, since I was the first in line, there wouldn't be anything in there. Boy, was I wrong! I started praying as I reached down further into the pot. Did you know, that thing was made in the shape of a funnel? As you can guess, my keys had gone to the very bottom of that funnel. As I prayed, "Lord, please don't let me throw up," I pulled them out. Now what? I took one of the liners and wrapped my keys up. "Now what, Lord?"

Praying again, I looked around, trying to find something I could use to clean off my hands and my keys. "I need help here, Lord," I said, continuing to pray and look around. To my surprise, over in the corner, there was a big bottle of hand sanitizer. It was one of the largest I had ever seen.

...I started questioning,
"Why had this happened? God uses so many things in my life to teach me lessons. What was this lesson?"

"Thank you, Lord," I said. As I reached down, I pumped some of the hand sanitizer into my hands and picked up the bottle. After cleaning my hands, I pumped it about three times to clean my keys. Then I cleaned off my keys, not one time, not two times, but three times for good measure. Then

I cleaned my arm, not one time, not two times but three times. If one time was good, three times was better. All the time, I was thanking God for the antibacterial soap and the fact that I was not vomiting. Then my hands got a good scrubbing again. After that, I rolled down my sleeves, picked up my keys, and I walked out of that Porta-Potty like nothing had happened. "I'm not telling a soul," I told myself.

A couple of days later, I started questioning, *"Why had this happened? God uses so many things in my life to teach me lessons. What was this lesson?"* In a still, small voice, it was like God said, "*Carla, so many times in yours and your ladies' lives, you have been in the Porta-Potty of life, all dirty and can't get clean on your own. You know, Jesus is the only way you can get clean. Just like the antibacterial soap setting over in the corner of the Porta-Potty, He's over in the corner, waiting patiently, wanting to clean you up."*

I told the Lord that day, "OK, God, I'll tell it every chance I get." Oh yes, I do tell my Porta-Potty story every chance I get, especially if it gives God the glory He so richly deserves!

8

THE LETTER

Cathie Paxson

When I was a young girl of 12 years old, I went to a Billy Graham Crusade. At the close of the crusade that evening, Dr. Graham gave an altar call. I had accepted Jesus as my personal Lord and Savior when I was five years old, but that night, I felt an overwhelming tug at my heart to go forward and rededicate my life to the Lord. As the crowd was singing, *"Just as I am without one plea, but that Thy blood was shed for me, and that Thou bid'st me come to Thee, Oh Lamb of God I come...I come."* I walked to the front of the auditorium to rededicate my life to Jesus.

A lovely, kind lady met me at the front and talked and prayed with me as I rededicated my life. As I was leaving, the kind lady gave me a slip of paper with her name and address on it. She told me to write her back someday and tell her how my walk with the Lord was going. When I got home, I tucked that slip of paper away in one of my drawers.

Many years later, I was cleaning my room, throwing old papers and things away. I suddenly pulled out that slip of paper from the kind lady. The memories of that night, so long ago, came flooding back into my mind. I decided I would write her a letter and tell her that the Lord was the most important thing in my life. I also wanted to thank her for taking the time to talk and pray with me those many years ago.

As I mailed the letter, I wondered if she had moved or would even get my letter. But to my surprise, several days later, I got a letter back! It was from her husband; he was a pastor. As I read his letter, the tears began to fall from my eyes. He told me that the very day they got my letter was the day that they buried their precious son. He was a soldier who had been killed in the Vietnam War. He went on to tell me that my letter was the greatest comfort to them on the worst day of their lives. He told me that they felt it was God's faithfulness bringing them comfort the very day they needed Him most. It reminded me of one of my favorite hymns, “Just When I Need Him Most..."

Just when I need Him, Jesus is near.
Just when I falter, just when I fear.
Ready to help me, ready to cheer.
Just when I need Him Most!

Just when I need Him Most!
Just when I need Him Most!
Jesus is near, to comfort and cheer.
Just when I need Him Most!

Just when I need Him Most, public domain

9

THE LAST PACK OF CRACKERS

Tammy & Curtis Sumner

The year was 2004, Curtis had been laid off from his job and we found ourselves moving from a small town in rural Alabama to the huge Metropolis of Minneapolis, Minnesota. This move was a big step of faith for us, but we embraced the Steven Curtis Chapman song, "*The Great Adventure*" as our theme song, and we set out on our own Great Adventure.

We were a young family; our children were just four and nine, and we had very little money, typically living from paycheck to paycheck and some weeks, relying heavily on the overdraft protection of our bank. Then came the layoff. Curtis searched far and wide for another job, but everything fell through, even the ones that he seemed certain to get. Then, a company from Minnesota, that we had not even considered, contacted him and offered him a job. We had felt the "winds of change" blowing for quite some time and had been praying for God to reveal where He wanted us to go, and we knew this was it.

As was usual for us back then, we left Alabama as broke as we could be. We had expected our house to sell and some checks to come in before our move, but, one by one, our plans had fallen through. So, we set out on the long drive to Minnesota trusting in God, praying that we were doing the right thing and counting the days until Curtis's next paycheck would hit. We had very little money and a lot of expenses, so we stopped at Walmart on the way out of town, and I cried as Curtis returned the bicycle that we had bought Lauren for her fourth birthday.

With our hearts sad but our hopes high, we arrived in Minneapolis. It was the biggest city I had ever seen and somewhat of a culture shock for this southern girl, but we were excited to see what God had in store. I spent the daytime hours looking for a house or apartment while Curtis worked. In the evenings we'd meet back at the hotel and spend time together as a family. Our son had temporarily stayed behind with my dad in Alabama and would join us once the move was complete. That was a blessing for the tough times that were to follow.

I had hoped, and we had prayed, but we didn't feel worthy of such a miracle.

That first paycheck took longer than expected to come in; our house still hadn't sold, and the bills were mounting. We were now out of money, out of food and out of gas, and almost out of time on our hotel stay. We sat in our minivan, holding the only food we had (a single pack of crackers left over from a salad some time ago). We bowed our heads and prayed for a miracle and asked God to bless that little pack of crackers because that was supper for our daughter that night; Curtis and I would do without.

After praying, I asked Curtis to go back to the ATM to check our balance, just one more time. I had hoped, and we had prayed, but we didn't feel worthy of such a miracle. Curtis slowly got out of the car and headed toward the ATM; his head hung low; sadness gripped his face. But when he checked the balance, there was money in the account! I remember seeing him walking back to the car with a spring in his step and tears in his eyes. Once again, God had provided for our needs; the company that had laid Curtis off paid him a bonus, a bonus that we never expected!! Just minutes before, things seemed hopeless, and we didn't know what we were going to do, but God made a way and instead of just a single pack of crackers; that night, we ate like children of the King!

Through that bonus, God provided enough means to cover the hotel and food until Curtis' first check and, soon afterward, our old house in Alabama sold, and there was more than enough money to meet all our needs. Through the years, God has been so faithful to us. It was this experience that led us to choose the name, "Faithful Crossings" for our ministry because we realized that day, more than ever before, that God is truly faithful at each and every "crossing" in our lives.

"Therefore, humble yourselves under the mighty hand of God, that He may exalt you in due time, casting all your care upon Him, for He cares for you. -1 Peter 5:6-7

10

WHEN DOCTORS SAID "NO"

ReJeana Leeth

I was born in 1965 with spinal bifida and club feet. I had my left kidney removed at the age of 2. I was in and out of Children's Hospital in Birmingham with many surgeries in the first few years of my life. By my 6th birthday, I was scheduled to start school, but I had both feet in a cast from surgery. I was so excited but not sure if I would start school on time, but I did. I had wonderful classmates that helped me carry my tray and books and awesome teachers who would help if I needed it. It was very hard, but I pressed on.

As the years went by, I started high school and never dreamed I would see those years. The doctors told me that by age 16, I would be in a wheelchair, but God kept me from that. In my senior year, I wanted to drive but wasn't sure I would be able to. The Driver's Education teacher called me by my first name and told me they had hand controls and were going to teach me to drive; I cried and thanked him. For a whole week, I was able to drive with my teacher and ultimately passed my test. I drove to my parents' house and surprised them! They had no idea I would be able to drive, but God showed up and opened a door for me through the school. My parents were so happy, and so was I.

The doctors told my parents that I needed to work on my independence and told them to let me do whatever I was able because one day, they would be gone. They followed those orders, and it ended up being a blessing, as now they are both in heaven. It was a reminder that God knows what we need in his time.

I have been using my voice ever since I was four years old. My Uncle Ray Mitchell and Pastor Shorty and Susie Dover taught me how to sing. They would work with me all week long and teach me a new song to sing for Sunday. I walked on crutches all my life, but they would help me up to the altar, and I would sing.

The doctors also told me that by the age of 20, I would be in a nursing home, flat on my back. But God had other plans. He allowed me to sing to those folks. I don't have time to sit aside, as he has done so much for me. I have had 33 surgeries.

I am very happy to wear this old body out because when I get to Heaven, I will have a brand new one.

The doctors told me that I would never be able to have children, but God had other plans. He blessed my husband and me with our first Miracle Child. She weighed 4lbs when she was born. Her name is Crystal, and she is 26 years old. Six years later, he blessed me with my 2nd Miracle Daughter Samantha she weighed 6lbs. Both Healthy. God has always brought me through every need and desire I have had. When the doctors said no, God said YES! I am now a grandmother never thought I would ever have children or much less be a grandmother, but God knew and saw my future.

I thank God for all the doors he has opened for me, my family, and friends that love me, and I love them back! There are bad days when I can hardly get out of bed and go, but you will never see that side. I am very happy to wear this old body out because when I get to heaven, I will have a brand new one. As the song says, *I've Got More to Go To Heaven for Than I did Yesterday.* My Faith and Trust is in The Lord. He is my strength that carries me each and every day. If you think of having a pity-party, look around; we are Blessed because people around us are suffering more than we are. My saying each day is I AM TOO BLESSED TO BE STRESSED.

11

THE PRAYER OF A CHILD

Tammy Sumner

Our little boy, Chandler, was about four years old and attending a nearby preschool while I worked as a music minister at a local church. One evening when tucking him into bed, it came time to pray. I asked him what he wanted to pray about, and he said, "*Mommy, I want to ask God to put water on the slide.*" Well, I wasn't sure what he meant by this, so I asked him for more details. Apparently, the slides were hot, and his legs stuck to them when he would go down them. He had decided that what they needed was water.

I explained to him that while it is very important that we talk to God and tell him what we need, that sometimes we don't get what we ask. In my heart, I couldn't see how this prayer would be answered, and I was hesitant to pray for it because I didn't want Chandler to lose faith in God. But Chandler insisted, "*Please, mommy, please pray for water on the slides.*" So, I bowed my head and began the prayer, as earnestly as I knew how, "*Dear Jesus, PLEASE let there be water on Chandler's slide tomorrow...*"

The next morning, we awoke to find that there had been a substantial, refreshing rain overnight. When we arrived at the preschool, Chandler exclaimed with perfect joy- "*Look, mommy! Water is on the slide!*" -Oh, that we would have the faith of a little child!

Chandler sliding with his big sister, Lauren

12

THE UNEXPECTED JOURNEY HOME

Johnathan Bond

I was asked to do a television show in Nashville and was leaving Chattanooga in plenty of time. But, because I am a planner by nature, I started thinking about driving 2.5 hours to the studio and being at the television station for 3 hours. That would mean 5.5 hours with no food, and that wasn't going to happen! So, I took the first exit to grab a meal. As I took the exit, I realized that this was the worst exit to get off for food in the Chattanooga area! There are only two fast-food restaurants on this exit, and one is extremely slow, while the other is extremely dirty! So, I had to make a quick decision if I would prefer risking being late to the studio or if I would prefer possibly getting a disease, and I chose the 'slow' restaurant. Just before turning into the parking lot, I asked GOD to please not let them be slow today, and then I noticed that the drive-thru was empty and said, "THANK YOU JESUS"!!

As I pulled up to the speaker, I heard, "*Welcome to McDonald's. Can I take your order?*"

I said, "*Yes ma'am, I will take a #2 with a Diet Coke, and that will be all.*"

She replied with, "*Thank you, that will be $11.88, drive up.*"

I said, "*Oh no, ma'am, I just want the Quarter Pounder meal.*"

She said, "*Yes, sir, that will be $11.88, drive up.*" I knew the order was incorrect but wasn't sure exactly how she had messed it up.

When I pulled to the first window, I said, "*Ma'am, I am only wanting a Quarter Pounder, medium fry, and medium diet coke.*"

I could tell that she was getting frustrated with me, and she said, "*Sir, your total is $11.88,*" so I just gave her a smile and a credit card, paying $11.88 with NO IDEA what I was about to be eating.

He smelled the food and knew that I was packin'

I pulled to the next window, and the lady handed me a drink carrier with two large drinks and a bag that seemed full. I sat the drink carrier over in the passenger seat and looked in the bag before pulling away. In the bag were three burgers and two large orders of french fries. So, I said, "*THANK YOU, JESUS!!*" I had 2.5 hours to drive, and I could certainly make this happen!

As I pulled onto the entrance ramp of Interstate 24, I noticed a guy walking, so I pulled over and asked, "Where are you headed?" He said, "Illinois," and I responded that I was headed to Nashville and would give him a ride if he wanted. He got in the car, and I felt a little bad because I had hidden my food. My wallet was in the cup-holder, but my food was protected! I asked if he had eaten, and he said, "*No, but you can go ahead and eat, I will be fine.*" He smelled the food and knew that I was packin'. I told him that I had extra food if he would like some. He said, "*why would you have extra food?*" It was that very moment that I realized that this wasn't a mistake at McDonald's, but a "GOD plan." I told him what happened, gave him one of the burgers and fries and a drink. We laughed and chatted while heading to Nashville.

As we were approaching Murfreesboro, Tennessee, I told him that I had a meeting scheduled in Nashville and asked where he would like me to drop him. He told me his preference, and I said, "*Now, that is on the east side of Nashville, and my meeting is on the west side. So, I will need to let you out around here, or you can go with me to my meeting. I will be at the meeting for about three hours, and then I can take you to the other side of Nashville, no problem.*" He told me that it is really hard to get a ride in the city and said that if he could go with me that he would appreciate the ride to the east side after the meeting.

As the television show started, they asked me to share my personal testimony, and then I was asked to sing the song, "*You Don't Know All That He's Done for Me.*" As I was singing the song, I looked over at this 29-year-old who was broken and emotionally overflowing with tears. IT WAS BEAUTIFUL! I love how GOD put us together for the greater good!

After the television show, we headed toward the other side of Nashville. On the way there, he said, "Do you mind if I talk with you on a personal level as we are driving?" Of course, I agreed. He said, "*I was raised in church like you were but, at 19 years old, my friends and I went to our parents and told them that we weren't interested in the Christian life and we all left. I woke up the other morning in Pennsylvania and looked around. None of my friends and none of my family was there. I thought to myself that it is time for me to go back home. I wasn't even going home for church, but because I need my family. However, maybe GOD has a plan for me.*"

I began to encourage him, telling him that GOD does have a plan for him and has had that plan even before he was born. I must talk more than I realize because, as we crossed into Illinois that evening, he said, "*My parents live about 30 miles off of this first exit, and don't know that I am coming. You can let me off at this exit if you want, and I will get a ride there tomorrow.*" I said, *"No, sir, you have come too far to stop now. Here's my phone; why don't you call them?"* I heard him on the phone say, "*Mom, I am 30 miles from home, can I come home, please?"* Although I didn't hear the other side of the conversation, I noticed tears in his eyes as he handed me my phone. I said, "*She said YES, didn't she?"* He was so excited.

As we went to turn in the neighborhood where his parents lived, I noticed that he had started tensing up, and I asked if he was okay. He said, "*I haven't seen my parents in almost ten years. Do you mind introducing yourself?*" He wanted me to break the ice for their reuniting. As we pulled up on the street in front of the house, his parents were standing on the front porch arm in arm. I walked up and stretched out my hand, saying to the dad, "*Hello, my name is*

Johnathan Bond." His dad hugged me and never said a word. His mother hugged me and cried the entire time. She said, "*You have no idea how long we have prayed for this day.*" I stepped back to allow space for the family to reunite. BEAUTIFUL!!

I love how GOD does what only HE can do! TOTALLY AMAZING!!

13

"WHO DOES YOUR HAIR?"

Melanie B. Greene

For as long as I can remember, my mother NEVER liked her hair. It was a long-standing thorn in her side. The fact that she had fine, thin, color damaged hair, that seemed to worsen with age, didn't help in the least.

As human beings, we define our beauty by what our culture deems beautiful, which usually is how we appear on the outside, without a glimpse of what's on the inside at all. Thank goodness we have a spiritual side and a God who views us in a COMPLETELY different way by COMPLETELY different standards! I love the quote that states, *"We are not human beings having a spiritual experience; we are spiritual beings having a human experience."* ~Pierre Teilhard de Chardin

I am especially reminded of two distinct verses in the Bible:

"I praise you, for I am fearfully and wonderfully made. Wonderful are your works; my soul knows it very well." Psalm 139:14

"Do not be conformed to this world, but be transformed by the renewal of your mind, that by testing you may discern what is the will of God, what is good and acceptable and perfect." Romans 12:2

My mother would literally walk up to a PERFECT STRANGER and ask, *"Who does your hair?"* During my teen years, it was somewhat embarrassing. However, as I grew older, it actually became something I came to love and appreciate about her. It was simply "HER WAY." She never met a stranger and loved everyone, whether she knew them or not. She was truly a loving and nurturing soul.

Don't get me wrong; we didn't always agree on things or see eye to eye. And, she had a temper that wouldn't be ignored, especially on the things she held close to her heart, like her daughter. I realize now that, through it all, she wanted to protect me from every hurt or unpleasantry that may occur from my actions and choices.

I am ETERNALLY GRATEFUL to God for blessing me with a "God-fearing" Christian lady that I was privileged to call my mother for 52 years of my life. Although she is with the Lord, she remains FOREVER in my heart. My family even says I sound like her at times. I'm a firm believer that we all become our mothers in a way. Although she didn't have perfect hair, she was the most beautiful of people from the inside out--the most loving and caring example of God's love a child could have or ever hope for in a mother.

14

AN INCREDIBLE ENCOUNTER WITH MY FATHER

Denise Fullerton

I realize cancer testimonies are common. Most everyone has been touched by it in some way, whether themselves, a relative or friend. What I want to share with you is how my Father, God, took this terrible, awful, very bad thing and used it for my good.

On October 9, 2009, I received a diagnosis of Multiple Myeloma Stage 3; this is a blood cancer that attacks and destroys the bone. I had no family history, no risk factors, wrong age, wrong gender, and wrong race according to research as to who is the most likely to have this type of cancer. I had never even heard of it, and yet, there I was. This diagnosis finally came after nine long months of unbearable pain, visits, and testing from five doctors/specialists; each gave up and sent me on to the next. Treatment ranged from radiation, chemotherapy, and steroids, to a stem cell transplant in August 2010. The most accurate description of the transplant is as one nurse described to me. She said they would be taking me to death's door, and God willing, bring me back. They did, and they did, by the grace and will of God.

I had suffered this unbearable pain for what seemed like a lifetime. I prayed " hard," as they say, all those months. I prayed for God to heal me and take the pain away. I told Him if He would do that for me, I would honor Him and praise Him and give Him glory for it the rest of my life. It seemed like either, He was not listening, or He was just not going to answer. I prayed. I read the scriptures. I searched for something, anything, to help my situation. Nothing.

I had read in scripture a few times about crying out to God with a loud voice. I decided that was what I needed to do. So I made a plan. I would spend the next day alone, in the quiet with no TV, no phone, no music — total silence. I asked God to search my heart for anything that might stand in the way of Him hearing my prayer or answering. He heard and answered for sure! All that day, as He brought to my attention different things; words I had said, thoughts I had, actions I shouldn't have done, things I should have said or done that I hadn't; I would stop and pray for forgiveness and help in turning from each thing He brought to light.

By the end of that day, I felt so clean and refreshed! The next morning, I was up early, heart pounding with excitement and fear! I like to think He was excited too. He already knew how this would go, and He had a beautiful gift for me that I did not know.

As I lay there, waiting for Him to speak, heal me, or take me home, I was surrounded with peace I had never experienced before.

I took a quilt and drove our utility vehicle out to a pond near the center of our 78-acre property. I thought I could cry out in privacy there. Spreading the quilt on the ground, I lay down before my Father, God, surrendering myself; I began to pray, thanking, and praising Him for all that He is and what He had done.

I shared with Him the pain and anxieties I had experienced over these months. I told Him I knew He was the Great Physician, the Creator, and that He had the power to heal me. I told Him that I trusted Him, and I was willing to accept whatever outcome He willed, whether He healed me completely at that moment or took me home to be with Him or left me to endure this pain the rest of my life. Whatever the outcome, I promised to lift His name in praise; to honor the name of Jesus and live to bring glory to Him for the rest of my life.

As I lay there waiting for Him to speak, heal me, or take me home, I was surrounded with peace I had never experienced before. It was as if the Holy Spirit became the atmosphere around me. Isaiah 43:1-2 came to mind: "Fear not! I have redeemed you. I have called you by name; you are Mine. When you pass through the waters, I will be with you; when you go through the river, you will not drown; When you walk through the fire, you will not be consumed, the flames will not scorch you for I am the Lord your God, the Holy One of Israel."

When I got up from that quilt, I knew He did not take me. I knew he had not healed me, but I knew He would be with me. I had a deeper trust and confidence in my Father than I ever had before.

I have been through the waters, the flood, and the fire. He has never left me. It's been ten years, and I am living life with very few limitations. If I had not gone through this trial, I might have never known Him with as much intimacy that I do today. I do not hope that you go through something like cancer, but I do hope that you will experience an incredible encounter with my father, God.

15

BRINGING OUR CHILD HOME

Emilee Ann Neal

God is incredibly faithful when you follow His will for your life; I am living proof of that.

If you knew me at the beginning of 2018, you would know, I did *not* want children. I was set in my ways and knew in my heart that I would never change my mind. On July 11, 2018, God changed my plans. It is funny how we make "plans." I'm sure God was laughing every time I said I was never going to be a mom.

That hot July night, while lying in bed, attempting to fall asleep, I had this feeling God called my husband and me to adopt a child. It wasn't an audible voice; it came through a simple feeling. Most people ask, well, then how did you know it was God calling you? My answer: I never wanted children, so a thought like that could not have come from me.

That night, as my husband was already asleep, I began to research everything about adoption. From "how to announce an adoption to your family" to "how to adopt a child," I felt like I knew everything after the four hours of research, but I was barely scratching the surface. After about one hour of research, I woke my husband up and asked, *"How do you feel about adopting a child?"* He halfway woke up and replied, *"sure."*

After two years of marriage, I wasn't sure he would say "*yes*" because of the countless conversations about how we never wanted children. The next day, I called him at work to see if he remembered the conversation. He said, "*Yes!*" He was ready. I think God was slowly preparing my husband's heart to want to be a father.

Without knowing the first thing about adoption, I called all the local agencies. Most were understandably too busy to get back to me right away. In the county where I live, there are over 2,000 children in the foster care system.

I called around for days, did more research, and spoke to my husband about options every chance I had. We decided to go through the foster care system to adopt. However, this decision was not made in prayer. We just assumed this was the best option because of our financial situation not being ideal (young college graduate with loads of debt). We waited for several days to hear back from someone at our local foster care system. We knew they were busy, so we tried to wait patiently.

I finally received a phone call after waiting for what felt like forever. The sweet lady on the phone was gracious to talk to me and answer all of my questions. I explained, "*We would like to foster to adopt a child under six years of age.*"

She replied, "*I might suggest you look a different route then. Children under six years of age are harder to adopt through foster care.*"

I thanked her for her time and quickly got off the phone call. At that moment, I felt like adoption wasn't in our cards. I cried for a bit and then called my husband. He was disappointed, too, but encouraged me that there would be a path, maybe that just wasn't it.

We could have let fear hold us back from God's calling...

We took a week to pray and research other options. It came down to a privatized adoption or an international. Anthony, my husband, was leaning towards a private adoption, and I was leaning towards international. So, we prayed fervently for a week. I prayed God would change one of our hearts, so we could fully be on the same page.

Sunday after church, Anthony said to me, "*I believe I feel God calling us towards international.*" And so, we began our process.

We had no idea where to start, so google became my trusted friend. After a couple of days, we selected our agency and set up a call with them. They spoke through all the fees, requirements, and what the process would look like. We didn't know which country to select but, thank God, we were only eligible for one country, Colombia.

We didn't know this at the time, but we would soon grow to love the country and the Colombian Culture, what a blessing to be led straight to where God wanted us and where our child is.

We filled out the application, and our agency accepted it within a couple of weeks. And thus, the official process began. As soon as you begin the international adoption process, the bills start coming.

We could have let fear hold us back from God's calling because the average international adoption is around $30,000-40,000. With blind faith, we jumped into this process, not knowing where a single penny would come from. By the grace of God, we have never once had to stop or slow the process because we couldn't afford a fee. Around $15,000 has been raised for our adoption as I write this. I look back in awe of how amazing of a gift this is, and we attribute every penny as a blessing from God. Our community has rallied around us to help bring our child home. As excruciatingly hard as an international adoption is, God has blessed us, provided for us, and guided us every moment.

When fear and uncertainty creep in, we look back on how faithful God has been to see us through this far, and we have confidence that He was, is, and will forever be faithful!

16

THE SEARCH FOR A GODLY WOMAN

Curtis Sumner

I joined the Marine Corps in the spring of 1988 after quitting college and working for a while. I just couldn't quite figure out who it was God created me to be. Music had always been a huge part of my life, but I floundered at college. I kept running into walls and obstacles that challenged my faith. At 19, I decided to follow my brothers into the Corps. The obstacles were larger; the pressure was stronger, the battle for my faith harder. I dated a little in the first years but never could find that right person.

The search for a godly woman was frustrating, to say the least. I finally gave up! I still remember that prayer like it was yesterday. "*Lord, I know you created someone just for me, I just don't know where she is. I am so tired of looking, and I'm leaving it in your hands.*"

Not too long after that, we were given a 4-day pass for Labor Day. It wasn't quite long enough to drive back and forth from North Carolina to Missouri, so my roommate invited me to go home with him for the weekend in Alabama.

I had spent some time in Georgia but had never been to Alabama, so I went. Saturday, we hung out with his family, and then on Sunday, we went to his mother's church-- *Friendship Baptist Church--* somewhere in the woods of Etowah County. They were having a "Singing with Dinner on the Grounds," which I had no idea what that even was! We walked in and there she was, singing with her family.

The way that service worked was they sang a little, then broke for lunch and then sang some more. Well, I made my way up to her during the break, and we talked a little, realizing every second that she was exactly who I had been praying for. My friend had other plans that day, though, and needed to go, so we left. A few miles down the road, I asked him if he could take me back to the church so I could see her again, and he agreed. When I walked back into the church, and our eyes met again... I knew.

They had another concert that night, and I helped load the equipment and said goodbye. My heart was aching! Finally, meeting *The One* and watching her leave, not knowing if I would ever see her again, was agonizing! I spent the next couple of hours sitting on the porch of an empty church in the heat of an Alabama summer thanking God and reflecting on what had just happened. John eventually came back for me (no Marine left behind), and we went back to Camp LeJeune. I called her often, and we would talk for hours. As often as I could, I went back to Alabama to see her. Now, after 27 years of marriage, she is still the godliest woman I have ever met, and my heart still beats a little faster when she walks into the room.

17

WHEN YOU LEAST EXPECT IT

Tammy Sumner

On a cool September Sunday in 1990, I stepped into Friendship Baptist church in rural Alabama. I was there to sing at a Homecoming service with my family group, "The Free Hill Singers." It had been a tough year for me. I was a freshman in college and had broken up with my high school boyfriend earlier that year, and I had lost my big brother in a devastating vehicle accident barely three weeks prior. This was my first concert since the funeral and, although my emotions and feelings were still pretty raw, I put on a smile. My heart had been broken, but I was trying to remain strong.

My Uncle Bill was a wise man. He was one of those rare people that could see into your heart and know what you were feeling; many times, when no one else could. On that particular day, he somehow knew I needed encouragement. Though I had said nothing to anyone, and no tears had been shed, he still knew. He sat down beside me on that old wooden bench and leaned over to me and in the quietness of the moment said something like this,

"Tammy, I know you are sad. I know you feel alone and want someone to love you. God has someone special for you, and if you will just trust Him and turn it over to Him, when you least expect it, there he will be."

As he was finishing those words, my Aunt Sue ran up and said, *"There are two little soldier boys back there!"* I turned around to see Curtis and his friend, John, sitting just a few rows back.

Our country was in the beginning stages of sending troops over to the Middle East for Operation Desert Shield, and it was an honor to see them at a church service, but there was something more to it. Something about one of those guys was different. I found myself looking at him time and time again, and he would always be looking back at me with a smile. As soon as the service ended, I anxiously waited to talk to him.

He was the shy one; yes, I made the first move. Actually, I believe our bass player, Dorothy, pulled him over to me, and THEN I made the first move! He complimented my singing, and I gave him my business card (it was so silly, but it worked).

God was busy bringing a young, Missouri boy... by way of the US Marine Corps, that day.

This Homecoming service was the old-fashioned kind. One of those "*all-day singings with dinner on the grounds*" type of services where you'd come together for a morning concert, then break for what would be considered a massive feast, followed up by more singing in the afternoon! I couldn't wait to see Curtis during lunch and saved him a seat next to me at the table. I wouldn't let ANYONE sit next to me the whole time. I waited and waited, but he never came. I eventually headed back to the sanctuary of the church and realized that he wasn't there either.

We were more than half-way through our second set of music when he stepped through the door at the back of the church, and my heart melted! That was the beginning of our love story… how unsuspecting I was of the plan that God was about to unfold before me that day. How sad and alone I felt on the inside and, yet, God was busy bringing a young Missouri boy, on his first trip to Alabama, by way of the US Marine Corps that day.

Maybe you are discouraged, and you feel that there's just no hope for you; God sees your heart, and He knows your hurts, your insecurities, and all the things that you hope for. Rest assured, knowing that if you place those things in God's hands, that He will take care of you.

Curtis & Tammy on their wedding day in 1992

Curtis & Tammy with two of their three children, almost 30 years later

18

PRETENDING IN THE PEW

Ralph Dorman *(as told by De Dorman)*

I had all the right answers and knew how to go through the religious motions of Christianity. I was even a deacon in a good, fundamental Baptist church, but if I had died at that time, I would have been sent straight to hell.

All my siblings and I were sent to church early on in life, which is a good thing. I was a regular in Sunday School class and knew each of the Ten Commandments. During a Sunday school contest, I even won a prize for memorizing the books of the Bible. I must have been sixteen years old when my parents came to watch my brother get baptized. During his baptism, a well-meaning person tapped me on the shoulder and whispered, "*Don't you want to accept Jesus as your Savior, too?*"

There was no conviction in my heart over sin, but how could I say no? I went forward during the invitation at their nudging, not the nudging of the Holy Spirit. As the altar worker showed me John 3:16, I was clueless as to what he was talking about, but when we got to our feet, he announced to the congregation that I had made a decision to ask Jesus into my heart. Should I speak up and tell them that I had no idea what had just happened, or should I be still? I was baptized soon thereafter, and so the charade began.

It went on for five years until one Thursday night during revival when an evangelist came to our church and preached on the text, Matthew 7:21, "*Not everyone that saith unto Me, Lord, Lord, shall enter into the kingdom of heaven,*" I knew that my heart was not right with God, and had known since the beginning.

If I stepped out now to be saved, what would my pastor say? After all, I was a deacon in the church. For that matter, what would everyone think if I went forward? It was a most uncomfortable feeling, as though the furnace at the church had been turned up full throttle. I remember gripping the back of the pew that was in front of me until my knuckles were white and throbbing. At the invitation, I felt that if I didn't respond to salvation, then I never would get another chance, so I stepped out and went forward. This time, however, it was the nudging of the Holy Spirit that prompted me, and this time, I understood what the altar worker was saying; this time, I had peace in my heart afterward.

I must admit that my pastor was quite shocked, but he handled things very well. Of course, I was no longer a deacon, and I was baptized again. But now I had His light to guide me. I wasn't pretending anymore. 1Samuel 16:7 says, "*for The LORD seeth not as man seeth; for man looketh on the outward appearance, but the LORD looketh on the heart.*"

19

WHEN GOD HAS A PLAN, HE MAKES A WAY

Les Butler

The year was 1997. My two great business partners and I were blessed to own Butler Mortgage in Kissimmee, Florida. All was going well. The business was booming; I had just built a new home on a lake for me, my wife, and two children. Both sets of parents lived within 5 minutes of our home. Can you say, babysitters?!

Through various events and circumstances, God had put a plan in place that would move us from our new home and successful business to Nashville, Tennessee, to run the start-up, Solid Gospel Radio Network. When I told my 11-year-old daughter we were moving, her response was, "I hate you, and I'll never talk to you again." To further complicate things, we couldn't sell our home. I knew the Lord was orchestrating this, and my wife and I had peace about it.

On the day of our move, the moving van drove up our driveway, and there was a car that drove in behind it. When the doorbell rang, I went to the door, and there stood my friend and mentor in the mortgage lending business, Les Murdock. He had recently passed his real estate license. In his hand was a contract to purchase my home. So, the movers started boxing up our belongings as I signed the contract.

God's faithfulness is beyond my finite, human comprehension! Since that day, God blessed me to lead the Solid Gospel Radio Network team, as well as the Singing News Magazine for almost 20 years. In recent years, I have owned Butler Music Group, Family Music Group, the Old Time Preachers Quartet, and have been called to preach the glorious gospel of Jesus Christ. I've produced, played and promoted tons of #1 songs, won awards, the blessings go on and on. I had no idea the Lord had all of this in store for my family and me.

You are probably wondering how things ended up with my daughter. In less than one week, she was voted the treasurer in her new school, and today she works for the *Singing News Magazine*, the very reason I moved to begin with, you just can't make this up!

20

THE CRIPPLED LAMB

Tammy Sumner

When our oldest son (who is now 24) turned 1 year-old and still had not cut any teeth, we became concerned and took him to his pediatrician. What ensued was a barrage of doctor's visits, tests, x-rays, and genetic studies that spanned over several months. The final word was that our beautiful, smart, and sweet little boy would never have any teeth. There were NO tooth buds and, therefore, there would be no teeth; not then, not ever. This diagnosis was, by no means, as bad as other sicknesses or deformities that some children have to deal with but, still, we were heartbroken for our sweet little boy.

We had named him, *Christian Taylor*, his name would tell the world "whose" he was, and we believed that God had great plans for him. So, we just trusted God that His plan was being worked out.

At bedtime, I would always sing Christian a song (or two), read him a book, and pray with him before tucking him in. He was almost two years old on that snowy December night as I pulled him close to me in his little white rocking chair and opened Max Lucado's book, "*The Crippled Lamb*," for the first time. It was a gift from my sister, Diann, chosen especially for my sweet little boy. It was a story about a little lamb that wasn't like all the others, BUT God had BIG plans for him, and He got to be there to witness Jesus' birth.

I was in tears as I finished this sweet story. I bowed my head and thanked God for His promise to do great things in Christian's life, and I once again prayed for a miracle. After praying, I felt a nudge from the Holy Spirit to reach into Christian's little mouth one more time, and when I did, I felt two little teeth! What a miracle! Just 4-5 months prior, the doctors and specialists said there were NO teeth and no tooth buds!

We had named him, Christian...

his name would tell the world

"whose" he was...

Over the next few months, Christian continued to get new teeth in until he had a total of 9! I know that's a far cry from the number most people have, but it was enough to attach a partial appliance to in the beginning, and, when he got older, it was enough to attach a permanent bridge! That wasn't the end of the miracles for Christian. The expensive dental work, not once, but twice, was donated by his dentists so that he could have a beautiful smile.

God is good, and I believe he still has big plans for Christian, and I believe that He has big plans for you. Be encouraged that God loves you. He knows what you are going through, and He cares, even for the crippled lambs.

21

WHEN FEAR COMES KNOCKING

Paula Breedlove

Did you ever wonder what happens during childhood to cause someone to develop a fear that they carry with them all the way through adulthood? Some remember the incident that was the root of their fear, and some don't. I am one of those that remember, and I remember it all too well.

I was one of those curious little ones who wanted to know what was going on downstairs after I was supposed to be sleeping, snug in my bed. About halfway down the stairway was a wall that hid me while I sat and eavesdropped on conversations that weren't meant for my little ears. There was one conversation that I heard more than once, and it would continue to haunt my dreams all my life.

It was my parents talking about some of my aunts and uncles who were dying or had died of cancer. The details of their suffering in the last months and final days could never be erased from my mind once I had heard them, and let's face it, you can run from monsters, spiders, and snakes, but you can't run from cancer. I never shared this fear with another soul, but from the first time I heard that word, I would pray this prayer every night at bedtime:

"Now I lay me down to sleep; I pray the Lord my soul to keep, if I should die before I wake, I pray the Lord my soul to take, and please God, don't let my mother, father, brother, grandma, grandpa or myself ever get cancer! Amen."

Throughout my life, cancer remained my greatest fear. As an adult, those fears became a reality. My grandmother was the first of my family to be diagnosed with breast cancer, and although she lived long after the cancer, she always struggled with an arm that was swollen to twice its normal size. About five years later, my mother was diagnosed with breast cancer and my father with cancer in his salivary glands. A few weeks following my mother's surgery, she was also diagnosed with ovarian cancer. Before it was all over with, I learned that one should never ask if anything worse can happen, because you might find out it can.

While my mother was in treatment, I had my first mammogram just to ease my mind. If my mother had not been sick, I would not have had testing done, and if I hadn't done that, I wouldn't be here today! When my cancer treatments were over, I had lived through my greatest fear. But now there were new fears- the fear of having the cancer return and the fear of cancer in family members; that was a fear I had yet to face. My mother's ovarian cancer returned after a few years and took her life. Without having a chance to grieve her loss, I became a caregiver to my father with the help of Hospice until he passed nine months later.

As bad as these three years in my life had been, cancer would eventually strike again. Ten years later, my daughter, who was only 32, became the 4th generation in a row to have breast cancer. Because I had been through it, I was able to be there for her in a way that not many could have been. Today we both remain cancer-free and participate in the Relay for Life. It has been over 27 years since my diagnosis.

As a child, my mother took us to church and Vacation Bible School. It was at a Church Christmas party that I had my first experience with making music. Before Santa would hand out gifts, we had to perform for him, and I chose to sing "*He's Got the Whole World in His Hands*," and it was a big hit! Following that performance, I was asked to sing in church. Now, everyone knows you don't need to have a great range in your voice to sing that song, and the pianist played songs right from the hymnals and never thought to change the key for my limited vocal range. I struggled through singing for a while because they said, "*If God gives you a gift that you don't use, he'll take it away*," and I certainly didn't want to lose the gift of my one-octave voice!

...let's face it, you can run from monsters, spiders, and snakes, but you can't run from cancer.

Despite my limited singing endeavors, I never gave up on my love of music. I wanted to be a part of it, and later in my life's journey, songwriting became the perfect place for me to make that happen. In my early thirties, I began to pursue songwriting seriously. In time, I was able to have a series of successes writing country, Gospel, & bluegrass songs. It wasn't till 20 years later when suffering from shingles causing vertigo so bad, I could hardly raise my head that my outlook changed. I lay there on my back with my iPad and wrote a lyric called "When Fear Comes Knocking;" this was the first in a series of miracles.

After my recovery, I met the Gospel, award-winning songwriter, Gerald Crabb, at the National Quartet Convention. He suggested that we write something together so, I sent him the lyric "When Fear Comes Knocking" as soon as I got home. The next miracle came a few days later when it was a finished song, co-written by Gerald and me! If that wasn't miracle enough, his son, Adam, had just joined the Gaither Vocal Band and took the song to Bill Gaither. It was recorded a few weeks later and will remain one of the most exciting events in my songwriter career! My faith kept me going for over 20 years to reach this place in my life.

It may sound strange to speak of God's faithfulness to me when the very thing I feared the most had come to be, but, if not for Him, I believe that the grief would have gotten the best of me. God gave me the gift of music that kept me going. People often say that God won't give you anything you can't handle. Well, I don't believe God gives people cancer. Cancer is just one of those bad things that happen, even to good people. God is the one who is there faithfully, helping us through it until the day we will be in a place where there is no such thing as cancer. Until then:

"When fear comes knocking, let Faith answer the door
When storm clouds gather, take shelter with the Lord
With your trust in Jesus, He'll be your shield and sword
When fear comes knocking, let Faith answer the door."

22

THE PEANUT BUTTER STORY

Penny Cook

During a season of my life when I was a single mother and struggling financially, one of my daughters came and asked what might seem like a simple request. She said, "*It's been a while since we've had any peanut butter. Could we get some*?" I told her I'd see what I could do about that, and she went off to bed. Well, I remember laying on the couch and crying like a baby because I knew there was no money to buy peanut butter; I had a good, old-fashioned, pity party. I cried out to God and told Him how unfair it was that my children had to do without such a simple request over circumstances that were not their fault. I told Him I felt ashamed to question Him and complain when we certainly had not gone hungry. Many friends and church family had been faithful to help us. God had shown His faithfulness time and time again. I told Him it surely would be nice to be able to go to the store and get not only our needs but also a few "wants" like peanut butter! I cried myself to sleep, feeling like a failure as a mother. (The peanut butter was just the straw that pushed me over the edge of much financial stress)

The next morning, I got up to run the Meals on Wheels route that I worked that summer. I took one of the girls with me every day, so I would have some special time with the daughter who went for that day. The same one went with me that day who had asked about the peanut butter. We got to one of the houses, and the sweet little lady who lived there asked if I could wait a minute after we had given her the meal. She went into her house and came back with a can in her hands. She then preceded to say,

---

I cried myself to sleep,
feeling like a failure as a mother.

"*I went yesterday to get my commodities, and they had this can of peanut butter in my box. Well, I don't buy peanut butter because it gives me "the gas;" I love it, but it sure doesn't love me! Well, I kept thinking about this can of peanut butter in my cabinet last night, and I got up and ate a spoonful. Let me tell you, that spoon full of peanut butter kept me up all night! When I got up this morning, I thought, I've got to get that stuff out of my house! Then I thought about you and your little girls coming by here every day. I don't want to offend you by offering you an opened can with a spoon mark in it, but I figured kids all love peanut butter. Would you mind having this can of peanut butter?"*

I'm sure she wondered why I was crying before she could even finish her question! Absolutely! We would love to have such a precious gift! In that moment, it was more valuable than a can full of gold! Sure, a can of gold would have bought a house full of groceries, but not the lesson my children and I learned that day and that we have never forgotten. God does hear our prayers; He hears our heart cries. He hears a little girl say, "*Can we get some peanut butter?*" when there's no money to buy it. That little lady could have given us a loaf of bread or a bag of potatoes. But it would not have been the miracle that God wanted us to have. It would have been appreciated, but not something that I would remember so vividly 20 years later.

My God is an awesome God, and He cares about me personally. He cares about you, too. Bring your needs and your concerns to Him. He will show you how big and loving and able He is. I've just always felt bad that the poor little lady had "the gas" all night to get our miracle to us!

23

GULF WAR PRAYERS

Tammy Sumner

What a year it had been. It was late fall of 1990; I had lost my brother in a devastating vehicle accident in August of that year and, soon afterward, had met Curtis, the man of my dreams. I had been on such an emotional roller coaster, but things were good and looking better.

It was almost Christmastime when we received word that Curtis would be in the next Marine unit heading out to the Saudi Arabian desert for Operation Desert Shield. I was devastated, just recently losing my brother, now risking the loss of the man that I believed God had made just for me. I cried, and I pleaded with Curtis to please find a way to stay home, but this was his duty; he had made a promise, and he would follow through with it. I knew I had to let him go and trust God to keep him safe.

Day after day, night after night, I sat glued to the TV, watching every news story that I could find. Praying with all my heart and hoping to get a glimpse of Curtis on the live footage. We would mail letters back and forth, but it took long periods of time to travel between us. I had found out that he was positioned just behind the front lines; it was his job to repair the guided missiles and lasers for those at the forefront of the coming battle. Desert Shield was quickly evolving into Desert Storm, and I was terrified!

During this time, I had a solo career and was asked to sing at a Nora Lam conference. Nora Lam was a famous evangelist & missionary to China. The major motion picture, "China Cry," was made about her miraculous survival in front of a Chinese firing squad. I found Nora to be a great woman of faith, and I talked with her, at length, after the event. I told her about Curtis being in Saudi Arabia, and she spoke to me about the power of prayer and gave me one of her books to read. I came home and immediately began to read, and I poured myself into daily, powerful prayers, asking for God's deliverance for Curtis and pleading for God to return him to America before the battle began.

I knew what it was like to lose a brother, mine had been gone for only five months, and that emotion was still so very raw.

I was at work that day when I received the phone call. While on duty, in his patrol car, Curtis's brother had a cardiac arrhythmia and had died. Curtis was already in-route home on emergency leave for ten days. Oh, how my heart ached; I couldn't hold back the tears. I wanted Curtis to come home, but I would have never asked for it to be in this way. I knew what it was like to lose a brother; mine had been gone for only five months, and that emotion was still so very raw. While my heart broke for Curtis and his family, I knew that God had answered my prayers to bring him home safely. The ground war started just after he got home and was over before he was due to return, so he was ordered back to Camp Lejeune and never returned to the war.

Sometimes God rescues you from the battle; other times, He walks through it with you. It isn't my place to ask why He chooses to let some live and others die, but I know that God is sovereign. I know He still answers prayers, and I know that even if you walk through the valley of the shadow of death, that He will be with you!

Curtis in Saudi Arabia, 1990
drawn in the sand is a heart with the words,
"I Love You Tammy"

24

CHANGE IS NOT A CHALLENGE FOR HIM

Ann Downing

Shortly after my husband Paul and I got married, we put together our singing group, The Downings. I had sung five years with Speers, and in the recent past, he had been with the Dixie Echoes. We had 23 years together before Paul went to heaven, and The Downings was a huge part of that marriage. I had never wanted to do anything but sing, so when Paul passed away, and there was no longer a singing group, it hit me hard as to what I was going to do. God had already opened doors for me to do some solo work and speaking. It was His way of preparing me, I truly believe. I began to get invitations to sing and speak, and now, in looking back, I know the way had already been made for the next season of my life. It is not the same, but I truly understand when the Scripture promises that He will fill in the blanks of our lives. I am still able to sing and speak, as I love to do. No, it is not the same, but there are myriads of ways to serve HIM. And He makes them all work when we give them all over to Him to create and lead. Change is not a challenge for Him!

25

PRAY WITHOUT CEASING

anonymous

My mother was told by doctors in the spring of 2017 that they would do everything they could for my brother, age 36 at the time, but that they could make no guarantees…

Rewind back to the time when he was 15 and in high school. That was probably the time we all suspected he was experimenting with marijuana or some form of drug. He was so rebellious then and so angry all the time. By the time he was 18 years old, he just seemed to want to live a life to please himself. He is nine years younger than me, and I just felt so helpless as I watched my baby brother careening toward a path of destruction, and my parents rescuing him from trouble, over, and over again. It was like one of those stories you see on the Dr. Phil show. Some years later, he had been diagnosed as bipolar, and to top it off, he became addicted to pain medications after a failed back surgery. Landing in jail for a week and being sent to complete a year at Teen Challenge by age 28 hadn't seemed to make any difference. My mom and I asked prayer warriors to pray. I knew my brother had asked Jesus to be His Savior as a teen boy, but I couldn't understand why, by 2015, my brother had become a full-fledged heroin addict. It was surreal. I think that was the point when my mom realized she couldn't help him anymore. An intervention occurred and, by God's grace, my brother agreed to go into in-patient rehab in another city that summer. The prayers were fervent for him during this grueling period of time. I begged God to save my brother. I know people in the family of Christ were praying for him, too.

In His divine mercy, God reached my brother, and he completed the intensive rehabilitation a year and a half later. During the time he was in rehab, my brother had decided on his own to return to church. He loved to worship at that church. It was undeniable that God was at work. When he returned home, he focused on living his day to day, trying to gain employment again. Church had once again fallen by the wayside. Looking at it from the outside, we were becoming a little discouraged. We were satisfied that at least he attended the Celebrate Recovery program and was able to find employment in the spring of 2017.

My Mom looked straight into the Doctor's eyes and said, "My son is not going to die from this." And then she prayed... fervently.

Not even one week into his new job, he became very ill. He had a very high fever and became delirious. The doctor's office that had ordered some bloodwork called the house and told my mom that my brother needed to go to the hospital right away. The diagnosis was sepsis. It was serious, and they couldn't find where it was coming from, and he was getting worse. The doctors who came in told my mother that people died of this, that they would do all they could but that they could not guarantee the treatments would work. My mom looked straight into the doctor's eyes and said, "My son is not going to die from this." And then she prayed... fervently. We all did. The people from my mom's church showered him with tangible expressions love as he spent his 36th birthday, weak in a hospital bed, and they bathed him in prayer.

After an extensive recovery time of a couple of months, my brother healed. The job he had just started that week he became ill, was held for him. Astonishing!

Fast forward to today, spring of 2019. Two months ago, my brother began serving on the worship team in his church, that church that had loved him and prayed him through his hardest time. Do I believe in a God who hears prayers, is faithful, and still works miracles today? You bet I do! He tells us in His word that "*...all things work together for good to those who love God, to those who are the called according to His purpose.*" -Romans 8:28. ALL of the things that my brother went through were not exactly things we can call good, but they were for the ultimate good, and for God's glory. I know God has a grand purpose for my brother and for all who call upon His name. I thank Him daily for the faithfulness He has shown to my family.

Do you have a loved one who seems doomed for destruction? "Pray without ceasing" 1 Thes. 5:17

26

BROKEN INTO BEAUTIFUL

Becky Miller

Divorce, especially in Christian circles, is a dirty word. It's the word we wish to ignore and sweep under the rug. The "unpardonable sin", even if you're the innocent party. I never expected to hear the word divorce applied to my life. Yet, statistics show that divorce, even among Christians, affects somewhere between 40-50% of all marriages. I never expected to be a part of these statistics. I never thought it could happen to me.

I was raised in a Christian home by two godly parents. The circumstances surrounding my divorce came out of nowhere. It knocked the wind out of me. I began to question why. Why me, God? Every day I would pray, "Lord, restore my home, bring peace." Even after my husband first left and the kids and I would gather for dinner, I would still set an extra place at the table. I still believed that my home would be restored, at least in the way I thought it should be, in the way that I thought was God's plan for my life. I never stopped praying. I never stopped believing.

Sometimes, however, God's plan is not always our plan. Often bad things happen and are beyond our control. They just can't be fixed, no matter how hard you try. Sometimes in life, things get broken. I was broken.

There are certain times in our lives when we just know that God is near; this was one of those times. It seemed God heard my prayers before I ever prayed them, knew my needs before I had them, and kept me in the palm of His Hand.

Times were hard. I often gathered my kids together to hold hands. I told them that I didn't know what the future held, but I knew we served a great God who promised in His Word that He would never leave us nor forsake us. I told them He had promised to meet our needs. Thankfully, I had a close-knit family, some amazing friends, a little church that loved on my kids and me, and an anonymous guardian angel.

During this time, I worked four part-time jobs. It took everything I had, with some help from my wonderful parents, to barely make ends meet. Amazingly, like the widow whose barrel was never empty, there was always enough. I remember the kids and I planning out a month of meals, clipping coupons, and making a grocery list to shop for bargains. I recall going to FOUR different stores in order to get the best prices for that month of meals. We stuck to the menu. It seemed the longer the month went; we still had food. We ate for almost two months on that food. God is good!

On one occasion, I received a cut-off notice from the electric company. It wasn't just an overdue bill, but a cut-off notice. I needed $90 to pay that bill the next day or my children, and I would be without electricity. I went to church that Wednesday night. I had scraped up enough money where I could pay the bill. When it was time to receive the offering that night, I knew I needed to pay my tithe for the week.

While the plate was being passed, I argued with God that I needed that tithe money to pay my electric bill the next day. I also knew that money was God's and not mine. God had always been faithful, and I knew He would not let me down. I wasn't sure how He was going to provide, but I knew I had to be faithful to God. Some people would call that irresponsible, but I had great faith that God would honor His Word.

God hates divorce,

but God loves the divorcee.

I put my tithe in the offering that night and prayed as it left my hand for God to make a way. I told no one that I had a need that night, not a single solitary soul. I told no one, but God. When I arrived home from church THAT NIGHT, I found an envelope taped to my door. I had no idea who it was from, but inside that envelope was exactly $90 cash — the exact amount of my electric bill. God was FAITHFUL!

Slowly, but surely, I began to heal. While I still have emotional scars that may never heal completely, God has lovingly gathered all my broken pieces, put me back on His Potter's wheel, and has reshaped and remolded me. He didn't just put me back together like I was, but He created a new me. Broken? Yes. Scarred? Yes. God has taken my broken pieces and made (and is still making) something beautiful out of it. What was meant to destroy me – what was meant to silence my voice – God is using in a greater way than I ever thought possible.

I thought my singing was over … BUT GOD

I thought my ministry was over … BUT GOD

I thought I would never find love again … BUT GOD

God hates divorce, but God loves the divorcee. I don't share my story to make you feel sorry for me; I share my story to encourage someone. You are not alone. You don't have to be a victim; you can be victorious. You don't have to live defeated; you can overcome.

Much like Job, God restored everything I lost and gave me more. God sent me a wonderful husband who loves and cherishes me. God gave me four bonus children that I love as my own. My husband and I often say we are not living in God's Plan B for our lives, but we are living in God's A+ plan.

Your story may be like mine, and it may be different, but most of us have been broken at one point or another. Remember, "ALL things work together for GOOD to those who love God, to those who are the called according to His purpose" (Romans 8:28)

27

GRANDDADDY WAS A PREACHER-MAN

Tammy Sumner The song, "Grace Still Calls," tells his story.

If you take a trip to Sand Mountain, Alabama, and mention my granddaddy's name, chances are you will still find many people who have fond memories of him. You would hear stories of the old camp meetings, revivals, and "all day singin's with dinner on the grounds." And you'd probably hear about a powerful preacher-man that had the boldness to proclaim the gospel, whether it be in a church, on the radio, or the street corner.

Yes, my granddaddy was a preacher man, one of the greatest I've ever known. He was the type of man who, to me, was larger than life. He was a tall man with a gentle face and kindness that radiated from him. He was a quiet man, except when he was preaching God's word with fervor and conviction. He was a man to be respected and admired. But there was a time that he wasn't like this at all.

Many years ago, when his daughters were young, my granddaddy was a drinking man, and when he'd drink, he would get mean. I've heard many stories, but the one that stands out the most is the time that he locked his wife and daughters in the old shed out back and went to get his shotgun. If it had not been for God sending the neighbor by to intervene, this story would have had a much different ending. As a matter of fact, there would be no story at all.

But God has a way of getting ahold of even the worst ol' sinner man. One day, while out in the woods, my granddaddy gave his heart to Jesus, and he was never the same. He put down the bottle and picked up the Bible and traveled around the countryside preaching and proclaiming God's word.

He was the type of man who, to me, was larger than life... a tall man with a gentle face and kindness that radiated from him.

Eventually, the daughters who were in the woodshed that day grew up to travel and sing about the love and grace of God, and one of those daughters was my mom. She taught me to sing, and now my family travels across the US singing about God's faithfulness. What could have been a tragedy ended up being a legacy. God still changes lives today. He still heals the broken, He still saves the sinner, and He still calls to you... why don't you say "yes" to Him today?

28

WAKE UP DANCING

Rick Boehm

I have suffered from multiple sclerosis for almost 17 years now. I was first diagnosed with general spinal maladies. The doctors prescribed a steroid infusion, and that helped my condition for ten years. After that, I had my next episode, and my new doctor diagnosed me with multiple sclerosis. This second doctor indicated that more than likely, my previous doctor misdiagnosed my condition originally. I truly praise God for those ten years as I was able to watch our youngest son play college and then NFL football. These last seven or so years, I praise God for allowing my health to be good enough to sing his praises.

God has also blessed me with my wife Deb, who continues to do almost all the setup, loading, and unloading of our sound equipment. My latest testimony song is "Wake Up Dancing." After my testimony, I finish with this line,

"Either here by a miracle from God, or when he calls me home, I know, without a doubt, I'm going to Wake up Dancing."

29

I'M HERE

Sally Abbott Quick

"I'm here."

God spoke those words to me when I was about five or six years old, and I have never been the same since. Let me quickly interject that I did not hear His voice audibly, but He spoke into my spirit in a way that was a combination of sovereign and precious that even a small child could understand.

I had been out riding my bicycle up and down the dead-end street where my family lived in Bradford, Tennessee. It was not "dead-end" in the sense of no future or hope, but just geographically because it was about a quarter-mile stretch of blacktop road lined with small mid-century houses on both sides other than a one-story red brick pajama factory at the end on the left. That long building is still there to this day. The factory was a constant source of contention between my mother and myself. Momma had given me and my three older sisters strict instructions to only ride our bikes on the street in front of our house and not on the access road behind the factory. And where is the first place a curious kid goes? Exactly where Momma said "not" to go. I spent a lot of time alone riding my green spider bike and thinking, so the scenery of that black strip of road occasionally got monotonous.

One day, I got the bright idea to zip around that long building on the left when I thought Momma wasn't looking. I quickly glanced back at the house to see if she was at the window. When I didn't see her there, I took off! I was peddling so fast that I was a little worried the chain might slip like it had done many times before. Any kid this has ever happened to, before elbow pads, kneepads, and bicycle helmets, knows that slipping a bicycle chain at top speed can be hazardous! I was not deterred by the potential of skinned knees or Momma's concerns at that moment. I made it successfully around the factory, probably in record speed, other than my neighbors David and Tommy, who won almost every race on that street. As I was peddling back towards home, I felt pretty smug about my victorious lap and the fact that I had supposedly gotten away with it.

I remember thinking, *"Ha-ha, nobody saw me; nobody's here."* At that moment was when I distinctly heard God say, *"I'm here."* I immediately looked up. I didn't need a theology degree to know who it was. While I felt the seriousness of the conviction, it was nothing compared to this extreme comfort that enveloped me, knowing that God was real and that He would always be watching over me. There was no fear. I didn't dread that God was going to take some legalistic vengeful guard over my every move but knew that no matter what happened from then on, I was safe in His care. He was watching. His loving presence flooded into my life and stayed beyond the day I realized who Jesus was. God has never failed me. God is ALWAYS faithful.

During the early years, God was faithful. I remember Miss Laverne's Sunday School class, getting my first Bible at age ten, and reading it all the way through just as she taught us. I didn't understand everything about the God of the Bible, but He was faithful just the same. God promised us in Hebrews 13:5, "*For He Himself has said, 'I will never leave you nor forsake you.'*" In Greek, this means that God will never let go, release, or neglect.

I remember thinking, "ha, ha, nobody saw me; nobody's here."

God stayed with our family when my twelve-year-old sister was diagnosed with a brain tumor, and for the next ten years as she fought and ultimately lost her battle. He was faithful when I drifted away as a teenager, and He was faithful when I came back to Him. He has been faithful through the loss of my Momma, Daddy, and grandson. He has been faithful through the gain of my precious daughters and granddaughters. God is faithful when people come and when they go. He is faithful when I sometimes lag in my walk with Him, and He has been faithful when I am pursuing Him just as breathlessly as I did while peddling around that pajama factory so many years ago. He was faithful then, and He is faithful now. How do I know? Because even though life has not turned out like I thought it would, life is still worth living when I'm living it with Him! There is nothing like waking up in the morning with an all-powerful, all-knowing heavenly Father who loves me and is working all things together for my good! The struggles and opportunities of each new day we face are no challenge for Him. My favorite line in a song I wrote called *It's a Sure*

Thing is "*I've put my hand to the plow, and I'm not looking back.*"

I have walked with God. I have walked without Him. I will never do that again. Not because I'm afraid of Him, but because I love Him. Because He loved me so much, He gave His son Jesus to die for me. I walk with Him because I can still hear Him say, "*I'm here*," and there is no sweeter sound.

30

THE GREATEST GIFT IS LOVE

Sandy Streicher Blair

"Ambrose, the doctor said the tumor is growing again."

"Can they do anything to stop it?"

"No, they can not."

"Does that mean I am going to die?"

"Yes, you are going to die."

A parent never thinks they will bury a child. That seems unnatural and odd. There is no "How-To Book" to do such a thing. But that is exactly where we found ourselves in 2017 when our eleven-year-old son was diagnosed and took radiation for a brain tumor. Trent and I decided to tell Ambrose that death was coming soon because he was about to face the HARDEST thing he had ever experienced in his lifetime. As parents, we wanted to disciple him and walk beside him to the very end. What I didn't realize was that he was to disciple us to the very end.

I love how God lifts up the weak to show Himself. I love how He uses the things we ignore to humble the proud. And I appreciate that He taught me the biggest pain I would experience in my lifetime would come from LOVE. Ambrose's death and our separation from him has given us such pain beyond what words can describe. In the book of Luke, chapter 2, Mary was told that a sword would pierce her own soul after she was told what Jesus was appointed for. Oh, how I now know what that feels like to have a sword pierce my soul. Walking the road of cancer and death with our eleven-year-old son, I now have a greater appreciation and value for love. Not the counterfeit "love" that the world gives. It is the LOVE that only Jesus Christ gave on the cross to redeem us.

That love was painful.
That love was unselfish.
That love was a gift that none us deserved.

Ambrose did not want to die. He wanted to earn his driver's license and marry his true love. He desired to have a wife and children one day, but that was not to be. Ambrose wiped his tears and got up each morning and invested in countless relationships. He poured love out on all who would take time to pay attention. It was all to end on November 14th when he breathed his last on this earth.

No one can buy that love. It is a gift. And even though my greatest pain came from love, I have come to realize that I have been blessed and truly feel like I am the richest woman on earth.

31

A PLACE CALLED GRACE

Sue C. Smith

I arrived for my co-write that morning, not sure how I was going to get through the day. Though I would be writing with good friends, my heart was aching, and my mind was racing with fears and questions. My daughter Jamie had called from Texas to say she was going into rehab again for addiction to prescription drugs. I will always remember her trembling voice when she said, "*This is the darkest place I've ever been.*"

This was something my girl had battled for several years, an addiction that began with back surgeries and well-meaning but ill-informed doctors who simply kept prescribing more pills even when she expressed concern that she was becoming dependent on them. Now the grip of this powerful force was threatening to destroy her, her marriage, and her children.

That day, my co-writers and I wrote a song called "*A Place Called Grace*." In the first verse, we used the line "*Now I sit here in the darkest place I've ever been,*" thinking of my daughter feeling so alone, and yet never abandoned by God.

That day was the beginning of Jamie's eventual deliverance and recovery. It was not an easy fight, but time and time again, I saw God's faithfulness to her, to her family, and to me. It would have been so easy for her church to ostracize her or turn away from her. Instead, she received cards and letters every day encouraging her and promising prayer support. It would have been expected for her daughters to be ruined by all they went through. Instead, God used the worst of situations to shape them into the godly women they have become. It would have been predictable for her marriage to have fallen apart. Instead, God strengthened her marriage and made it better than ever. Today every time I think of her, I thank God once again for His incredible faithfulness to His children

32

WHAT A CHANGE!

Jacqueline J. Williams

Having come from a family of eight kids, we had a good family life. Dad worked for JE Dunn Construction as superintendent for 18 years, and he had a partnership and his own business until he retired. Our family didn't attend church as a family when I was young; however, the church bus would pick us up each week for Sunday services. Mom would go with us on occasion and on holidays, but dad always had a reason he wouldn't go. For quite a long period of time, dad was doing a job for a minister named Don Barron, building the Ramada Inn, which was close to the airport. Don's mother "Grandma Barron" visited the job site regularly, always inviting my dad to their church, Tiffany Fellowship. She was very persistent, which is what it would take to ever get my dad to go to church. He finally gave in!

One evening he came home from work and said, "*Well, that same lady came by again today, and I think we're going to have to try her church, so she'll leave me alone & quit bugging me!*" The whole family attended that next Sunday, and my dad was saved! From then on, we attended every service. Dad and mom helped build onto the church by purchasing "church bonds," and Dad used his construction skills to help with the actual structure. So many were praying for my dad and our family. I know my sister, and I prayed each week that our dad would get saved! What a change!

My dad gave up the things of this world to serve God completely! He played his guitar, sang, and even wrote songs for God. Dad passed away on Good Friday in 2012. We continue to hear of people he helped with money or a musical instrument. What a joy it is to know that we will see him again in Heaven, thanks to Grandma Barron. She persevered and never gave up on my dad. We are blessed because of dad's decision to follow Christ that day!

33

THE MAN IN WHITE

Tammy Sumner with special insight from Robbie Sue Morgan
"It's Not a Miracle to God" tells her story.

Back in the 1960s, my mom and dad were in the prime of their lives. Both were in their 30's with young children, a home, and a long life ahead of them. Life was good, and they were happy. But one day, my mom became extremely sick. She couldn't breathe, her body was failing, and no one, not even the doctors, knew what was wrong. Her physician had heard about a rare disease called "Hamman-Rich Disease" and flew to New York to consult with some renowned specialists in the field. When he returned, he had confirmed that his suspicions were correct; she indeed had this devastating illness.

At that time, there were only a hand-full of known cases in the US and little to no survivors with no cure in sight. She was told that slowly, her lungs would fill with fluid, and she would "drown." At best, she would only have six months to live.

My dad went to my grandparent's home to tell them the news that their daughter was dying. He wasn't a Christian at that time, but my granddaddy was a preacher and a great man of God. He immediately said, *"Let's pray, Pete!"* My granddaddy prayed a powerful prayer that day, and he got up, praising the Lord and shouting all over the living room. He looked at my dad and said, "*We've got the victory over something, Pete, I don't know what, but we have the victory!!!!*"

Over the next few weeks, my mom grew weaker. The disease had begun to take a toll on her body, her fingertips were blue and swollen from the lack of oxygen, and she was so weak that she couldn't even raise up from her pillow. It seemed that the end was fast approaching. The pastor from the local church visited several times, and on one of his visits, my dad was saved! Soon afterward, when my mom was at her weakest point, she opened her eyes to see a man dressed in white standing beside her bed. He reached out and took her hand, and, from that moment, she began to recover.

Mom lived for another 40-plus years. Even her doctor gave God the glory for her healing! She out-lived that bleak diagnosis, and she lived to see her kids grow up, get married, and have families of their own. Most importantly, she never failed to testify and witness to others about the miracles that God had done in her life.

Tammy's mom & dad 40+ years after her diagnosis

34

YOU WERE BORN TO DO SOMETHING SPECIAL

Chelsea Estes

Have you ever just known that you were born to do "something?" Have you ever known that "something" has been inside of you before you even knew you had it, or that it was special? Have you ever vowed to use that "something" to share the word of God with whoever was willing to listen? This is a story about the gift of song, and the devastating trial I faced after I declared to use my "something special" for God.

I had the most wonderful childhood ever. I was raised in a loving, Christian home with my father, mother, and brother. My father is a Baptist minister, a man's man, with a hard, outer shell, and a heart of gold. My mother is as beautiful on the inside as she is on the outside and taught me how to be selfless and humble. My brother and I had a "love/hate" relationship when we were kids, but, as adults, he is my biggest fan and greatest supporter.

I have sung ever since I could talk! No exaggeration! One of my earliest memories of wanting to sing at church was in preschool when I sang, "Jesus loves me" with one of my best friends at church. I haven't stopped singing since.

In my adulthood, my mother encouraged me to make a Gospel music album, and with the help of a family friend, I made my very first music to call my own. "Who Will Stand for God" was released on March 10, 2017. I had singing appointments almost every Sunday that spring and summer. I had sung in church, weddings, and funerals my whole life, but this was different; I had my own music ministry to share the word of God, and I was on cloud nine! It really felt like life couldn't get any better than it was.

That July, my world came crashing down. I had been married for four years when I was faced with devastating facts that I knew in my heart had been true for a long time. My marriage was over. Satan knows when we are at our strongest. He also knows exactly where to attack you, when to attack, and where it will hurt the most. I was devastated. I didn't want to eat, I couldn't sleep, I didn't want to talk to people, I didn't want to be seen, I didn't even want to go to church, and I most definitely DID NOT want to sing.

I was mad at God, and I was at the lowest I had ever been in my life. Satan was filling my head will all of these lies, and I believed every one of them. He might as well have been looking me in the face telling me, "You're not good enough, you're not pretty enough, you're not fit enough, you're not perfect enough, and you'll never be ENOUGH!"

I turned to the only one that I knew could help me when I was ready to let it all go, and that was God. All I can remember is getting on my hands and knees and praying, "God, please give me peace!" After that, it was like all those feelings just melted away. I had a sense of calm and assurance that I know only my God can provide.

I was mad at God, and I was at the lowest I had ever been in my life.

I turned to my church and my family; oh, thank God for them both! I knew they were not only praying for me but for my husband, as well. God and God alone gave me the strength and the courage to continue to sing through my trial. Not only did he help me feel strong enough to sing, but to further my music ministry and pursue another Gospel album.

I promised God that no matter what happened in my personal life, I would never stop singing his praises and telling others about his love and the sacrifice he made for us to receive salvation. God blessed me through that trial, and after six months of separation, my husband and I received marriage counseling and worked together, through God's help, to renew our marriage.

Now, it has not been a bed of roses ever since, but whose marriage is? The most important thing to remember is that God is not the only one who pays attention when you are doing the Lord's work. We must be strong in the Lord and ready for the attacks from Satan when they come because they will! We serve a God who will carry us through anything if only we will ask him.

The title of my latest gospel album, "Daughter of The King," is not a coincidence. I want all you young ladies and women to know that you ARE beautiful, you ARE loved, you ARE smart, you ARE kind, and you ARE a daughter of the King! I want you to know that you ARE good enough, and to never, ever believe anything else! I am so glad that God made me the spunky, fiery, petite, southern gal that he did! He knew that's what it would take to tell the ladies of the world that HE is love, and the man that will someday profess his love for you must know God first to love you the way that God intended for women to be loved. AMEN! This is what I intend to do with my "something special," and with God's help, I'll do it in a mighty way!

35

LORD, NOT MY SON!

Cheri Taylor

During the last 25-30 years, I thought I had grown into a rather strong Christian woman who was fiercely dependent on God. I had become, and still am, a student of the Word! My prayer life had grown, and still is, constantly! As a born-again believer in Jesus Christ, I thought I had it all together until a phone call changed everything.

One afternoon I was working in my home office when the phone rang. The very kind man on the other end introduced himself as *"Sergeant Parker from the United States Marines"* and said that he was trying to reach my son, Philip Taylor. I quickly responded that he was not there, so the Sergeant asked if I would have him return the call. In shock at this ludicrous request, I quickly said: "*Son, you DO realize you're speaking with 'the Mother', don't you?*" His answer was soft as he chuckled to the affirmative.

Just as that conversation ended, my son, Philip, sent me a text simply stating that he had something he needed to discuss with his dad and me. At this point, he had no clue that "Mr. Fancy Pants" (Sergeant Parker) had called and left a message with this momma bear. My return message was this: "The MARINES?!?!?!? Don't you sign a thing!!!!" My phone quickly rang, and he asked, *"How did you know?"* My reply was, *"I'm the mom; that's why!"*

My mind was swirling through this brief conversation as I heard phrases like "*this is something I need to do*" and "*this is what I want to do.*" I really can't remember as those moments became a blur. After we hung up, I fell to the floor and curled into the fetal position and cried like a baby. All I remembered saying was, "*Lord, not my son! Please, not my son!*"

Next to the Lord, my husband, Greg, is my rock and comforter. He was not excited about Philip's decision but understood, much more than I, why this made sense. Our son was trying to find his purpose and, since college wasn't working out, this seemed like a logical step. I still wasn't convinced, and the tears were constant that evening.

After a fitful night's sleep, I got up just as the sun began to peek over the horizon. Sitting on my back porch, it was time to have a serious "one on one" with the Lord and convince Him that this military thing was all wrong. Although I could not hear Him audibly, the conversation was very clear, and it went something like this; *"Lord, I'm so thankful for all the men and women who are willing to sacrifice their lives for our country! I'm completely sincere when I thank them for all they do! But Lord, why my son? I can't do this! LORD! I only have ONE SON! Please, not my son!"*

Very gently, I heard His sweet answer, *"I, too, have just one son, and I gave Him for you."*

"Yes, Lord," I said.

He continued, *"Don't you think I can take care of that boy anywhere on this earth just as well as I can take care of him here?"*

"Yes, Lord," I whispered

He then responded, *"Then what's the problem?"*

My answer? *"I'm still the mom!"*

I wish I could tell you that I faced the next four years with nerves of steel and a faith that never wavered, but there were days I would lose my resolve and melt in a pool of tears. I would quote scripture for assurance and cry out to the Lord constantly. Psalm 56:3 says, "When I'm afraid, I will trust in You" but, I must admit to you, my dear reader, yes, I was afraid, and I was having major trust issues! However, God is still faithful, even when I'm not. He knows me perfectly, and when I fell to pieces, He held me. He never left or forsook me in my pitiful state, and He kept his hand on my son, as well.

As Philip's unit prepared to ship out for the Helmand Province in Afghanistan, I could barely speak. America was at war, and he was heading right into the heart of it! His dad and I knew that he was about to experience things most of us only hear about on the news but never see with our own eyes; this was getting too real. But once again, God is faithful. Little by little, His peace would settle on me.

During his deployment, I remember on two separate occasions telling the Lord that I just needed to hear his voice. "God," I said, "You know exactly where that boy is right now and what's going on, but I don't. I need to hear his voice to know he's alright. Is there any way you could have him call?" Just like my God, He proved His faithfulness, and within the next few hours, the phone would ring, and I heard the sweetest words any mother could hear during a time like that.....*"Hi mom!"* Thank you, Lord.

I haven't mentioned my sweet husband, Greg, much in this. He has his own story to tell of God's faithfulness. But I can assure you that he was on this roller coaster of emotions right alongside me, crying out to the Lord on behalf of our son as well. Perhaps one day he'll share.

America was at war, and he was heading right into the heart of it!

Philip is home now and safe. He's happily married with two children, trying to live the American dream. For that, I praise the Lord often! God IS faithful! This time, my story has the happy ending I prayed for, and God answered. As always, He kept his hand on our entire family during that time. I have to admit that I'm thankful for everything we went through because my relationship with the Lord became sweeter and deeper. He taught me more about Himself than I ever knew, and I continue to grow.

But what about the men and women who don't make it home? Does that make God unfaithful to them? A thousand times, no! He is always faithful even when lives fall apart. We live in a fallen world where sin abounds, and people die. I'm not assured of my next breath. But because I know I'm a born-again child of the King of Kings, He is FOR me!

36

MY MIRACLES

Carla Harris Justice

It was a beautiful, sunny day in January, but cold. I looked in my rear-view mirror after pulling out of our driveway to see behind me, a line of cars, trucks and a moving van driving down the road. All of us headed to Collinsville, Alabama, back to Mother's. I should have been relieved, but all I felt was numb. Numb to the past few days, numb to the past year. How could things have gotten so out of control? I remember thinking as I drove, "Well, I guess God is through with me now." That was the last thing I wanted after being a Christian since I was 7 yrs old. Here, I was a 45-year-old woman, starting over again! I remember asking myself, "Why?" "What was going to happen to me?" and "Where was God leading me?"

My husband and I had been married for 24 years. We went to a diet doctor to lose weight. Both of us went. I only took one pill!! I was mopping my 24' x 24' beauty shop for the third time. I hated to mop, so I knew something was wrong. Remembering the diet doctor told us not to stop taking the pills "cold turkey," I called my pharmacy. He laughed after asking me how many I had taken. I responded, "one." He said he thought I would be ok. Just don't take any more. I found out they were fen-phens. I've always watched out about taking medicines, so I didn't take it anymore. I told my husband, but he wouldn't stop taking his and wanted mine.

I started noticing things, things like phone calls with hang-ups if I answered. Unexplained drugs in his pockets or money missing. Too many fox hunting trips or used car sale trips to Nashville. You get the idea. It started with hateful words from him, then shaking me, yelling, then slapping. Telling me, he wanted me dead and then choking me till I passed out. I don't feel like I need to go into the "really bad things" because my ex-husband and precious daughter are still alive. Let's just say that it was deadly, but by the Grace of God, I got out. I made up my mind; I was going to serve God, no matter what. It's a wonder I got out without going insane. I was kicked down, BUT with God's help, I was not kicked out!!!!!!!!

After being at Mom's a little while, I started back to college and finished getting my degree in Human Services and a minor in Drug and Alcohol. I started to CrossPoint Church in Gadsden, AL, in the year 2000, and after going there for a short time, it was announced that a lady at the church was starting a Jail Ministry and needed ladies to go with her. As I made way to speak to her, I thought my heart would beat out of my chest. That's the way the Holy Spirit showed me something was about to happen. That was April 2003. I tell the Ladies in the Jail that was God working! I've been going to jail now for 16 years as of this past April. I've seen many ladies saved and working for the Lord. The devil has tried to defeat me, but God has protected me, time, and time again.

My miracles started when I was seven years old, and I got saved. Another miracle was when my husband planned to do me harm, and God protected me. Yet, another miracle was Isaiah 61; "He has sent me to heal the brokenhearted, to proclaim liberty to the captives, And the opening of the prison to those who are bound; To proclaim the acceptable year of the Lord." God called, and I answered. I was CrossPoint Jail Ministry Director to Etowah, Calhoun and Cherokee County Jails and St Clair Prison. I'm still Director of Carla Justice Jail Ministry.

I have said many times, "If God never answered another prayer, I have been highly favored and blessed," and that's another Miracle.

37

THE CHANGE IN ME

Daryl L. Haley, Sr.

After hearing the Reverend Earl Abel preach the gospel, I gave my life to Christ at around 12 years old, but I never regularly read the Bible. In fact, I lived a life where you would not have been able to tell that I was a Christian at all. Instead of following God's word, I chose to live like my friends around me. Although I knew many of my decisions were wrong, I went down the wrong path anyway. Even though my family and I went to church somewhat regularly, it didn't seem to affect how we lived our lives daily. I only knew how to do spiritual things because someone told me, not because I read it in the Bible The only reason I believe that I was saved is that God took care of me and answered some of my prayers, even though my times of prayer were rare. 2 Timothy 2:13 says, "If we are faithless, He remains faithful, for He cannot deny Himself." There were times when I felt called to change my life, but I would make empty vows to the Lord instead.

One of my vows was, "Lord, I'm going to come, but first let me find my wife." At the age of forty-two (after another failed relationship with a woman), I was a man who drank heavily, partied, and had multiple relationships with women, but I had met one woman and followed her to church. The church I was attending had started studying Rick Warren's book, *The Purpose Driven Life*. The book asked questions about how I was living for Jesus and had scripture to back up the questions. I finally cried out to the Lord, "Lord, I'm going to do it your way!" From that point forward, the Lord started drastically changing my life.

The Lord led me to start reading the Bible daily. I stopped leaning on my understanding. Proverbs 3:5-6 says, *"Trust in the LORD with all your heart and do not lean on your own understanding. In all your ways acknowledge Him, And He will make your paths straight."* The Lord led me to stop drinking; then, he led me to celibacy. I had struggled with my finances, and the Lord led me to tithe and to trust Him, (which is another testimony in itself). The Lord was and is molding me into his image, just as his word says that he will.

Even though my family and I went to church somewhat regularly, it didn't seem to affect how we lived our lives daily.

The prayer to live "the Lord's way" was in 2003, and by March 2004, the church I was attending asked if I would go with them on a mission trip. I was surprised and didn't know why they wanted me to go; I didn't sing, and I did not preach. So, I prayed to the Lord, *"I don't know why they want me to go, but I can get off work, and if you want me to go, I'll go, Lord!"* I went on the mission trip to Cedarville, Ohio, and while I was there, a friend introduced me to my future wife,

Janice Bolden. Janice was celibate, also, and had recently told her friends that she was going to start dating again. Praise the Lord!

Janice and I married in May of 2005, and the Lord has continued in growing and molding both of us. The same friend who introduced me to Janice also asked me to go through some discipleship lessons with him. I have been discipling men and women, along with Janice's help since 2005. The major change in my life is because of reading and applying the word of God!

I have been walking with the Lord for sixteen years, and my life is totally different than it was in 2003. Not only has the Lord changed my life, but he has also changed my only biological son, Daryl Jr., and led him to follow the Lord. He married his wife Lucretia three years ago, and I have a fifteen-month-old granddaughter named Delaya (which means "God has raised"). Praise the Lord!

Last year, the Lord led me to retire from the Post Office after twenty-five years of service and ten years of military service (another testimony). In August of last year, the Lord led me to start Bible College, on scholarship no less. I'm learning to teach God's word boldly!

I have problems and troubles just like everyone else, but the Bible teaches me how to live in a way that they are not self-inflicted and how to deal with the problems that happen. Matthew 28:18-20 says, "And Jesus came up and spoke to them, saying, "All authority has been given to Me in heaven and on earth. Go therefore and make disciples of all the nations, baptizing them in the name of the Father and the Son and the Holy Spirit, teaching them to observe all that I commanded you; and lo, I am with you always, even to the end of the age." Praise the Lord!

38

SIMPLE BLESSINGS

Tammy Sumner

It had been a very "full" year for our family. My father in law had passed away earlier that year. Then, Curtis took a new job, and we moved across the state to be closer to his family. This move was an expensive one for us with closing costs, moving expenses, and a new school for the kids (along with a pricey band trip to pay for). In addition to financial stresses, we were mentally and physically exhausted. Curtis's new job required him to travel to Minnesota in December of that year and, although funds were tight, we thought it'd be a nice opportunity for me and our youngest son, Chandler, to get away for a week. So, we packed our bags and headed out for the great North!

We arrived in Minneapolis late and went straight to bed. Curtis would have a busy day the next day, and Chandler, and I would have a fun day of exploring the Mall of America. That night, while we slept, a heavy snow covered the ground, and when the morning came, we awoke to a winter wonderland. I decided that Chandler and I would take the hotel's free shuttle service to the mall since the weather was less than ideal for driving. So, we bundled up in our warmest winter clothes and hopped aboard the small passenger bus, ready for an exciting day of exploring.

It was only a short ride and, before we knew it, we were stepping off the bus at a special hub just a few yards away from the massive mall's entrance! Excited, we walked quickly toward the mall, not realizing that the entrance in front of us led straight their huge indoor amusement park! I knew about the amusement park but had NOT planned on taking Chandler even close to it. The carnival rides and coasters would be too expensive for us, and I didn't want to have to tell him that he couldn't ride.

Once inside, Chandler's eyes grew wide, taking in all the bright lights and activities as we passed by. As I had expected, he began begging to see the rides. "*Please mommy, please can we go in?*" My heart ached because I knew I couldn't afford for him to ride. I finally agreed to show him around only after making sure he knew that we couldn't stay.

When I turned around, she was gone; just as quickly as she had appeared.

We had walked only a few steps when I felt a tap on my shoulder. I turned to see a pretty young woman with a smile. She said, "*I have an unlimited ride wristband, would your son want it?*" I immediately thought that it was a marketing ploy, or maybe there were "strings attached," but she assured me that she just wanted to give him the ticket. We accepted, and I bent over to put the wristband on him and to tell him to say "*thank you*," but when I turned around, she was gone, just as quickly as she had appeared.

My sweet little boy who had been content just to walk through and see the rides had the TIME OF HIS LIFE that day... and to top it off, just about an hour before we left, a little boy walked up to Chandler and GAVE him a souvenir. I talked to the mother, and she said her son just wanted to do something nice for Chandler.

That day, God smiled on this precious little boy of mine. Chandler will never forget the kindness of a stranger, and I will never forget how God sends blessings no matter how great or small our need.

Our day spent in the Mall of America Amusement Park

39

IT DIDN'T TAKE GOD BY SURPRISE

Bob Sellers

Well, my whole life is evidence of God's faithfulness. I had no idea what to expect when I left The Kingsmen, I'd never left a job without having another "real job" lined up, but I've been blown away by how He has blessed me and my ministry. It's hard even to put it into words, but I'll give you a couple of examples.

Within a week of leaving The Kingsmen, I'd received no less than seven job offers. I didn't want to pursue any of them, but each one felt like an affirmation straight from God as if to say, "*See, my child? You prayed and received peace for stepping out on faith, now here's the evidence that I'll take care of everything. You don't have to be scared to death anymore!*" And then the solo dates began to roll in, and I was booked through the end of the year in just a matter of weeks. I'm able to be home with my family when I want to be and manage my own schedule as opposed to being bound by someone else's.

Furthermore, without ever requiring a certain amount from any church, God has blessed me financially. An interesting turn of events from very recently is a great example of that. A church where I was scheduled to sing on Sunday morning decided to fire their pastor (the one who booked me) and cancel the Sunday morning concert at 9:30 the Saturday night before it. I had driven 9 hours and was already in town at the hotel when I found out! Well, thankfully, the room had been prepaid, and it was very nice, so I had a relaxing night and got to sleep late. While setting up my product table for that Sunday evening's concert, I found several hundred dollars in my cash box that I didn't know I had. I almost took a lap around that church! See, the cancellation took me by surprise, but it didn't take God by surprise!! He's a big, great, loving, wonderful God, and I count it a blessing to be able to stand on platforms all across this country and proclaim His goodness, grace, and mercy.

40

I'M STILL BLESSED

Ashley Marie Evans

My sister Brittany and I are twins. We were born on November 2, 1998, at only 24 weeks and were given less than a 10 percent chance of survival. If we had been born 1-2 years earlier, they would have let us die; they didn't save many babies that were born in 1996-1997 who were that premature.

At birth, I weighed only 2lbs, 2.5oz, and my sister, Britt, was only 1lb, 13oz. We were in the NICU and were allergic to almost all antibiotics. Lack of oxygen during the c-section caused us to have cerebral palsy.

Our biological mom wanted to keep us, but she didn't know how to take care of us. Her husband had died in a shooting over drugs, and she had just gotten remarried, so she chose to put us up for adoption.

My adoptive parents, John and Sheri (I will refer to them as "Mom" and "Dad" through the rest of my story), had wanted to adopt and were looking into it when they heard about us from some close friends. Mom's brother, Arthur, had cerebral palsy, and she had seen just how bad some nursing homes were, and she didn't want me and my sister to die or end up in a nursing home. So, Arthur inspired her to adopt us. We were adopted at three weeks old.

We had PBD, multiple brain bleeds, retinopathy, and hydrocephalus of the ventricles (incurable). We were too sick, in the NICU, to have a shunt placed, so we had to wait until we were older and stronger. So, when we were seven years old, Mom took us for an MRI to see if we would need a shunt. When they put us in the MRI, the doctors and nurses were amazed because the hydrocephalus was completely GONE!

I can hear and feel pain during my seizures, so I listen to music, which includes A LOT of Southern Gospel music. They help me by giving me, Jesus. They comfort and calm me in pain or during the seizures.

Now, out of all these medical problems, I'm still blessed. I believe that God put this storm in my life for a reason. When I'm weak, I get stronger in Him, and I am thankful that I'm alive and not worse off; this is how God makes something good from something that could have been way worse! I'm so thankful for all the amazing blessings, good or bad, because He will use my storms for another blessing in life. My life is awesome!

...a note from the editor

Ashley Marie is a vibrant, young lady who is living and loving life, even with many disabilities. When asked about her medical diagnosis, she submitted a list that was almost a full page long; yet, she is quick to give God the glory! She loves and lives every day to the fullest and is an inspiration to many. The scripture that she clings to when times are hard is, "*And we know that all things work together for good to them that love God, to them who are the called according to his purpose.*" -Romans 8:28

The following is a list of Ashley Marie's diagnoses:

Cerebral palsy
Hashimoto's disease
Non-epileptic seizures
Hypersensitivity to pain
30% deaf
Hypothyroidism
Asthma
Cornea transplant recipient
sensory neuropathy
Raynaud's syndrome
Palmoplantar hyperhidrosis
Sensory processing disorder
Out of socket elbows
Ulcerative colitis
Irritable bowel syndrome
Gastritis
No Gallbladder
Moderate hearing loss
Hip impingement
Hyperglycemia
Cataracts

Ashley Marie and twin sister, Brittany

41

GOD STILL WALKS ON WATER

Tammy Sumner

I was just a kid, probably not even in middle school yet. Although I was young, I was saved and really close to God. I remember going outside during those hot summer days and riding my bike and talking to Jesus. Some kids had imaginary friends…I had Jesus! We lived on "Leota Lake," a backwater lake of the Coosa River and I loved the water so much that I swam for hours almost every day. I had learned to water ski, and our family enjoyed being out on the lake, so we decided to take the boat out for a spin. I grabbed my skis and headed to the boat with my mom, dad and big brother, David. We spent some time out driving around the river, seeing houses and how the recent rains had caused flooding and left driftwood and debris in the yards. Finally, it was time to ski.

My big brother, as most big brothers will do, got ready to test me to see if he could drive better than I could ski. We zipped up and down the river as fast as that big ole pontoon boat could take us, and I held my own. I was feeling pretty good about myself. Mom and dad were talking and enjoying the ride with my brother, and then it happened; because of the high waters, he had driven straight into an area of stumps that were hidden just beneath the water. These jagged stumps were covered so well by the swollen river that you couldn't see them until you rolled right over them! I was still on my skis and knew that if I fell, it could cost me my life. So, I did the only thing that that I knew to do; I talked to Jesus. Now, I know that sounds silly to some of you, but it's the truth. It was what came naturally at that time in my life. There have been other times since then that it wasn't what came naturally. Instead of talking to Him, I chose to go to friends or other family members, or I even tried to "fix" things on my own, all of which ended pretty poorly but, this time, my response was to talk to Him.

I can't tell you how many stumps my skis glided by- maybe 20 possibly 30 or more, but I can tell you this; I never fell. I never even came close! This was not a testament to my skills; I was just a kid, and those stumps were too numerous and too close together. The odds were against me, but I was talking to The One that defies all odds; The One who is able to save. The One who rescues and redeems! If only we could talk to Him more and make Him the first place we go when there's trouble, then how much different could our outcome be? He's promised in his Word to never leave nor forsake you. So, whatever your problem is today- even if it feels like you will fall, even if it feels like it will end your life; let Jesus carry you through it.

"Be strong and of good courage, do not fear nor be afraid of them; for the LORD your God, He is the One who goes with you. He will not leave you nor forsake you." Deuteronomy 31:6

42

HIDDEN TREASURE

Lori Watwood Walker

Oftentimes in life when people cross our path, we have but a moment to make their acquaintance, making the meeting seem insignificant or irrelevant. But, occasionally, life's journey can bring along someone who changes our perception of life and opens the door of wisdom and true purpose. They can open our eyes to see people through Heaven's perspective.

Ms. Evonne was a dainty, unassuming little lady, often overlooked by many people. In many ways, she was like a lamb; humble, precious, and a bit insecure but easily led. At first glance, one would be tempted to only see a quirky, odd lady with a shy smile. However, if you looked with the eyes of your heart, you would find a beautifully anointed prayer warrior who could move Heaven with her faith.

Praying for people was a lifestyle for Ms. Evonne. When she felt led to pray for someone, she would simply ask if she could do so. It did not matter if it was on a weekday in Wal-Mart or church on Sunday morning. The first time I met Ms. Evonne, she visited the church my husband and I were pastoring. She came into my life at a point when I was experiencing unprecedented discouragement. This tiny, lamb-like lady made her way to me after service and began to explain how, within a three-week period, she had randomly met and prayed for five women at different locations within our city, all of whom were a part of our congregation. She felt this was a sign from the Lord, leading her to join our church. She then asked, "Would you mind if I pray for you?" With one eyebrow lifted and no words on my tongue, I slowly nodded my head 'yes ma'am.'

Without hesitation, Ms. Evonne began to pray the most lively, heartfelt, refreshing prayer anyone had ever prayed over me. It was as though this lady was throwing me a lifeline in the middle of my stormiest sea. I felt as if Father God himself was whispering in her ear, and all of Heaven came to back her up. In that moment, my eyebrow lowered, and my spirit stood up. I knew without a doubt; Heaven had brought me a treasure. It was wrapped in this tiny-framed lady most people would have avoided because they would not have taken the time to really hear all she housed in her heart. Ms. Evonne was a deep well. Everything about her life signified simplicity, and humility. She truly understood the scripture *"... by this we perceive the love of God, because He laid down His life for us. And we ought to lay down our lives for others..."* I John 3:16 NKJV

I felt as if Father God himself was whispering in her ear, and all of Heaven came to back her up.

I realized very quickly this lady was a true friend of the father. He brought her to me as a gift, much like a second mother. She was someone He wanted me to honor, love, and cherish as the jewel He had cultivated her to be. I asked the Lord to let me see Ms. Evonne the way He saw her. I soon learned this was a prayer He would always answer. She taught me through the life she lived what it looks like to let Him love others through my heart. When I rely on His love to flow through my heart, it never takes anything away from me. Instead, it always adds something to me. She demonstrated with ease how beautiful a surrendered heart is to the Father.

My husband and I, being pastors, understand we don't get to choose who we pastor. We pastor those who choose us. Some will allow us to really love them, and occasionally, some will love us in return. Ms. Evonne loved me in return.

I took every opportunity the Lord gave me to spend as much time with her as I could. For five years, she helped the Lord cultivate my heart for my life's purpose. She poured more love, compassion, and acceptance into my heart than I could possibly contain. I came to realize my purpose on this planet was to do for others what she was doing for me. Simply allow Him to love others through me without boundaries, and He would give me an endless supply of love to draw from. She has inspired me to love deeper, pray more, and lay my life down for the Lord like never before. My life has been completely changed.

On a sunny afternoon in March, with all her family and those dearest to her heart surrounding her bed, she lingered between heaven and earth. Her breath was shallow but peaceful. We all knew she was preparing to take flight. Her heart longing to see the Father, our hearts not ready to let her go. Nevertheless, we sang her favorite song and worshiped the Lord for the gift we had received from her life of faithfulness. As we raised a hallelujah around her bed, the presence of the Lord filled the room. In all His splendor, He came and received for Himself His beautiful, precious daughter. She had persevered and finished her race well. She left her family a legacy of love, and she will never be forgotten.

The most valuable lesson I learned from Ms. Evonne was to really look at people with the eyes of my heart, because I may be looking into the face of a true friend of God, and they just might change my life if I let them.

CONCLUSION

OUR STORIES, HIS GLORY

Webster's Dictionary defines a valley as "a long depression between ranges of hills or mountains." Today, I understand exactly what that means. But there was a time when I had no idea that the human heart could experience as much pain and heaviness as mine did and survive to tell about it.

Within a two-year span, I lost two uncles, a sister, a brother, my father, and a very close girlfriend. I also endured my second pregnancy, which was extremely difficult. The heartache and pain I felt was so great that at times I felt no pain at all. I was numb, completely numb. Even in all my agony, I was still able to read my Bible, pray and journal every day because I knew that the only way I would feel again was to spend time with Jesus. The only way I could get through two years of depression was to spend time with Jesus.

It was during this period in my life—the deepest, darkest valley I had ever walked through—that Bill Gaither would call on me to sing "God On The Mountain." It was, I believe, a divine appointment that God gave to me, a divine message I was desperately in need of. There are songs, and then there are *songs*. "God On The Mountain" is one of those songs.

God has promised that He would never leave or forsake us and that He would guide us with His eye. Isaiah 42:16 says, "*Along unfamiliar paths I would guide them.*" That means that even in the valleys and mountaintop experiences of our lives, God is always with us. His plans are for our good (Jeremiah 29:11). He surrounds us with His love and His presence, and even in the darkest times of our lives, we are not alone.

So, as you've read these stories of triumph and tragedy, my prayer is that you have been encouraged and know that the same God who helped these saints will deliver you. Knowing this, you can find peace in the midst of adverse circumstances and trust God for the victory.

—Lynda Randle
singer, songwriter,
author & TV personality

TOPICAL INDEX

Stories in this index are listed with two reference numbers, separated by a / mark. The first number, **in bold print**, refers to the chapter or story number (found at the beginning of each story, at the top of the title pages). The second number refers to the page where the story is found.

MINISTRY INDEX

The following is a list of the ministries represented in this book. If you are needing prayer, Christian counseling, or would like for one of these ministries to come to your church, please reach out to them directly.

Aaron Wilburn.........songwriter, humorist, singer, speaker aaronwilburn.com

Adam Borden....................Evangelist Adam Borden, evangelistadamborden.com

Ann Downing....................................Ann Downing Ministries, anndowning.com

Ashley Marie...facebook.com/tyehhbhxn

Becky Miller..............................The Millers, millermusicgroup.org 540-664-2470

Bob Sellers Ministries...........................bobsellersministries.com, 205-337-9997

Carla Justice Jail Ministries..carla.justice@tds.net

Cathie Paxson............................CEO GospelTown Records/Songwriter/Manager
Sweetwater Revival, SweetwaterRevival.com

Chelsea Estes Ministries...........chelseaestes.com, facebook/chelseaestesmusic

Cheri Taylor Ministries....... cheritaylor.org, cheritaylor@pcsi.net 812-549-8199

Curtis Sumner................Faithful Crossings, faithfulcrossings.com 573-721-7144

Jacqueline J Williams...............Sweet Spirit Ministries, sweetspiritministries.org
sweetspiritministries4@gmail.com

Johnathan Bond.. johnathanbond.com, 423-280-0547

Les Butler.........................Old Time Preachers Qt, oldtimepreachersquartet.com

Lorie Walker............................Summit Church, daystarsloriewalker@yahoo.com

Lynda Randle Ministries.....................................lyndarandle.com, 816-792-5353

Paula Breedlove...............................songwriter, facebook.com/paula.breedlove

Penny Cook......................Bible Teacher, Speaker, Writer, Tree of Life Ministries
ablessedpenny@aol.com

Ralph Dorman & De Dorman.....................songwriter, randddorman@juno.com

ReJeana Leeth & New Grace................................rejeanaleethandnewgrace.com
leethandassociates@gmail.com 256-364-9216

Rick Alan King Ministries.......................rickalanking.com, rick@rickalanking.com
615-855-1184

Rick Boehm..New Shoes Qt, newshoesgospelmusic.com
rickdeb@hotmail.com 712-325-6935

Sally Quick..sallyquick.com 615-403-0047

Sue C. Smith........................songwriter, Write About Jesus, writeaboutjesus.com

Tammy Sumner............Faithful Crossings, faithfulcrossings.com, 615-782-9293

ADDITIONAL RESOURCES

Addiction
Celebrate Recovery....................................celebraterecovery.com

Crisis
Focus on the Family Counseling..................focusonthefamily.com
Helpline..1-855-771-4357

Divorce
DivorceCare...divorcecare.org
DivorceCare for Kids..dc4k.org

Grief
GriefShare..griefshare.org

Family
Focus on the Family.....................................focusonthefamily.com

Finances
Dave Ramsey ....daveramsey.com

Pastoral Care (counseling/care for pastors & their families)
Care for Pastors...careforpastors.org
Care for Pastors' Kids...pastorskids.org
Hotline..352-728-8179

The resources listed on this page are ministsries that we have found helpful in our own lives and want to recommend to you. We have not been paid or compensated in any way and there is no affiliation between Faithful Crossings and the ministries and resources listed above.

This book is an outreach of

Faithful Crossings Ministries

Sharing the songs and stories of God's faithfulness to His children

www.faithfulcrossings.com

Made in the USA
Monee, IL
01 September 2022